Tracking
Marco Polo

TIM SEVERIN

Peter Bedrick Books
New York

By Tim Severin

Tracking Marco Polo
Explorers of the Mississippi
The Brendan Voyage
The Sindbad Voyage
The Jason Voyage   624151

Black and white photographs by
Michael de Larrabeiti

First American edition published in 1986 by
Peter Bedrick Books, New York.

93 92 91 90 89 88 87 86   1 2 3 4 5 6 7 8 9

Library of Congress Cataloging-in-Publication Data
Severin, Timothy.
    Tracking Marco Polo.
    Reprint. Originally published: London : Routledge &
K. Paul, 1964. With new introd.
    1. Severin, Timothy. 2. Voyages and travels—
1951–   . 3. Polo, Marco, 1254–1323? I. Title.
G490.S476   1986   910′.92′4   85-21418
ISBN 0-87226-012-7

Manufactured in the United States of America
Distributed in the USA by Harper & Row

Printed on acid-free paper

CONTENTS

PREFACE

THIS IS THE STORY of the Marco Polo Route Project, an attempt to re-trace Marco Polo's overland journey across the length of Asia. Half of Polo's long road now lies within the Chinese People's Republic whose borders were closed to the Route Project team, so that the theme of the Project is not yet entirely fulfilled. One day I hope it will be possible to travel the Chinese section of the old caravan road, but for the present this account concerns Polo's travels from Venice to the Hindu Kush. Across Turkey, Persia and Afghanistan, the three members of the Project team endeavoured to follow the exact path of the Polo caravan; to compare Marco's descriptions with our own; to unravel some of the mysteries which surround his narrative, and to enjoy ourselves in the process. Because of these aims, it may seem that wherever we travelled nothing had changed since the Middle Ages. This is not so. Great development has taken place nearly everywhere. But we were much more interested in uncovering the few unchanged facets of Asian life, and in concentrating on these scattered medieval relics it is easy to create a false picture of the countries concerned. At the same time I cannot claim that we tackled the problems of Marco Polo's Asia with any academic skill. Our approach was amateur. We possessed only the most elementary scholarship, gleaned from the mass of material written on the subject of Marco Polo. Our sole advantage was derived from personal experience of the same countryside which Polo had described nearly 700 years earlier. But this, after all, was the spirit of the Marco Polo Route Project.

From start to finish of our trip the idea of following Marco

Preface

Polo would never have been put into action had it not been for the assistance of many people. Elsewhere there is a list of those organizations who helped us with essential supplies of all kinds, and I should like to state that their liberality was very deeply appreciated. Here I want to take the opportunity of expressing our gratitude to that formidable body of sponsors who were kind enough to devote valuable time to our cause, helping us with advice, finance and recommendations. This group numbers General Sir Alexander Galloway; Warden A. Farrer; Professor C. Hinshelwood; Professor J. Needham; Col. Sir Tufton Beamish M.P.; Peter Roy Esq.; Cdr. A. Courtney M.P.; F. E. Harmer Esq. C.M.G.; Sir William Hayter; Professor E. W. Gilbert; C. G. Smith Esq; R. Saggars and the late Mr. Temple.

These names by no means complete the list, for in addition there were many people, in England and en route, who came most generously to our aid. To these therefore I say—thank you.

Oxford,   T.S.
February, 1964.

FOREWORD

The letter came from the man who was to be the editor of this book. Would I like to call at his office in London? He had read a magazine article I had written about my experiences in southern Persia looking for the trail of Marco Polo, and he would like to discuss the possibility of my writing a book about my travels. The publisher's office turned out to be a ramshackle warren of narrow twisting stairways, uneven floors where walls had been knocked through to make extra space, dingy cream and brown paint, and distracted inhabitants who vaguely directed me through the labyrinth, and then disappeared like absent-minded mice into cluttered holes.

The appointment was for 11 a.m., and I knocked at several wrong doors before finding the right office. "Come in!" I pushed open the door, and stood there. "Can I help you?" asked the scholarly looking man behind the desk.

I hesitated. Another wrong door, I thought. "I'm looking for Colin Franklin's office."

"I'm Colin Franklin," the man replied politely. "What do you want to see me about?" He seemed to have no idea why I was there.

"You asked me to come and see you at eleven," I explained, "It's about my magazine article."

He looked very taken aback. "But when I read the article and wrote to an address in Oxford, I was expecting a retired Indian Army colonel. Who had perhaps visited Persia on his way back home." I was twenty-one, and still a student of geography at Oxford.

So, from the outset, *Tracking Marco Polo* was both an

old-fashioned, and an undergraduate, book. When the type-script was accepted six months later, it encouraged me to continue with post-graduate studies in the history of exploration and discovery, and to try to make my living as a writer on the subject. In that way I hoped to be able to continue to make the sort of journey which formed the purpose of the Marco Polo Route Project and which I had enjoyed so much.

Now, twenty-two years later, a great deal has altered in the places which Stanley, Mike and I visited light-heartedly on our battered motorcycles, and yet I'm sure I would make the same decision again. Paradoxically those countries which we found easy to visit – Persia and Afghanistan – are now out of bounds to the casual traveller. But the country which we longed to visit but could not – China – has increasingly opened up to visitors. Turkey, meanwhile, has developed and industrialized dramatically. Excellent roads now run where once our motorcycles skidded and bucked on gravel and pothole tracks; and it seems that each provincial town now boasts its factory chimney where formerly we were greeted as such outlandish creatures that the Turkish shepherds set their dogs on us and, once, a particularly aggressive individual whipped off his heavy, greasy flat cap and skimmed it like a discus at Mike's eyes as he drove past and nearly brought him crashing off his machine.

Six years after my first visit to Istanbul with the Marco Polo Route Project I went back there. I managed to track down Irgun, the chirpy young Turkish entrepreneur who had befriended us and introduced us to his splendid Turkish family living in the poorest quarter of Istanbul. As I expected, Irgun had done well in the interval. He had gone off to Germany, worked in a factory there, and saved enough money to return home and open a souvenir shop just near the Istanbul Hilton. "The shop is very good business," he told me cheerfully, "We sell everything the tourists want." I pointed out a cabinet in one corner displaying an impressive selection of antique-looking coins from classical Greek and Roman times. "That belongs to a friend of mine," said Irgun. "He rents the space from me. If you want to buy any coins, ask me first."

"Why's that?" I asked.

"I can get you a better price," promised Irgun, "and many of the coins are fakes. My friend has them made specially. Last week there was a conference of some professors in Istanbul, and one of them came into the shop. He had a big reference book of coins with him, and he came back three times and looked through all the coins before he bought five of them to take back to a museum in his own country."

"And were the coins genuine?"

"Two were," replied Irgun with a grin. "But three were fakes. My friend made them only a month ago. You see, he uses the same reference book."

Of my two travelling companions, Stanley went on from Oxford to become in turn a poet, a trainee with the World Bank, an international civil servant and a Euro MP. Mike, meanwhile, was obviously sufficiently impressed by the easy-going lifestyle of his two undergraduate friends to decide that university life was worth sampling. He gave up being an assistant film cameraman, obtained a place at Trinity College Dublin, transferred to Oxford, and is now a successful novelist. As Stanley has also written ten books, it means that the former members of the Marco Polo Route Project have produced a total of more than twenty-five books between them. Clearly, besides their love of travel, they also shared an irresistible urge to set pen to paper.

For me, the events of the expedition foreshadowed many future experiences. Re-reading this account of the adventures, mishaps, and shear fun of the motorcycle journey along Marco Polo's path, I can recognize many features that were to recur. My later travels would also involve the same last-minute scramble to get everything ready for departure, and introduce the same bizarrely naive errors in the rush: how on earth could I have attached the two sidecars on the left, English, side of the motorbikes when setting out on several thousand miles of road where everyone drives on the right (or middle)? And I always seem to have had the same good fortune in the nature of my travelling companions and the people we met along the way.

But perhaps the most remarkable foreshadowing in *Tracking Marco Polo* is my interest even then in the sea road to the Indies. Specifically in this book I referred to the Arab navigators and their ships, and how Marco Polo was so wary of their vessels, because they were sewn together with coconut cord instead of fastened with nails, that he refused to sail in them. I had no way of knowing in 1961 as I hopped along the beach of Bandar Abbas in south Persia with a broken foot, and looked at the local traditional ships with their turbanned crews while the sweat poured down the wooden shafts of my crutches, that twenty years later I would organize the building of a medieval sewn ship and make the Sindbad Voyage, seven and a half months under sail from Muscat to China. For even then I was only following once again the genius who had first sparked my interest in re-tracing the journeys of exploration, because Marco Polo had made that same voyage, in the reverse direction, as he came home to Venice to tell the world about the wonders of Cathay.

TIM SEVERIN

Co. Cork
September 1983

ACKNOWLEDGEMENT

The Marco Polo Route Project was lucky enough to receive unstinted support from many firms and individuals. Their help was vital to our venture and I hope that they will feel that they shared in the success of our trip. These supporters were:

Anne Brown, Queen Elizabeth College, London.
B.S.A. Ltd., Birmingham.
Bryant & May Ltd., London.
D. Byford & Co. Ltd., Leicester.
British Bata Shoe Co. Ltd., Tilbury.
Courtaulds Ltd., Manchester.
Colibri Lighters Ltd., London.
Cascelloid, Birmingham.
Cadbury-Fry, Birmingham.
Champion Sparking Plug Co., Feltham.
Richard Costain Ltd., London.
P. B. Cow (Li-Lo) Ltd., Slough.
Cygnet Film Productions Ltd., Bushey.
Benjamin Edginton Ltd., London.
Garrard Sidecars Ltd., Bletchley.
Horne Bros. Ltd., London.
Horlicks Ltd., Slough.
Embassy of Japan, London.
Lacrinoid Products Ltd., Essex.
Joseph Lucas Ltd., Birmingham.
Mather & Crowther Ltd., London.
Marmite Ltd., London.
Midland Bank Ltd., Lewes.
Morlands, Glastonbury.
Royal McBee, London.
E. B. Meyrowitz Ltd., London.
Oxo Ltd., London.
Pascall Ltd., Mitcham.
P. & O. S. N. Ltd., London.
R. & J. Pullman Ltd., Yeovil.
Ridgeways Ltd., London.
Rolls-Royce Ltd., Derby.
Streetly Mfg. Co., Ltd., Sutton Coldfield.
Scott & Bowne Ltd., London.
H. F. Temple, Oxford.
J. Walter Thompson Co., London.

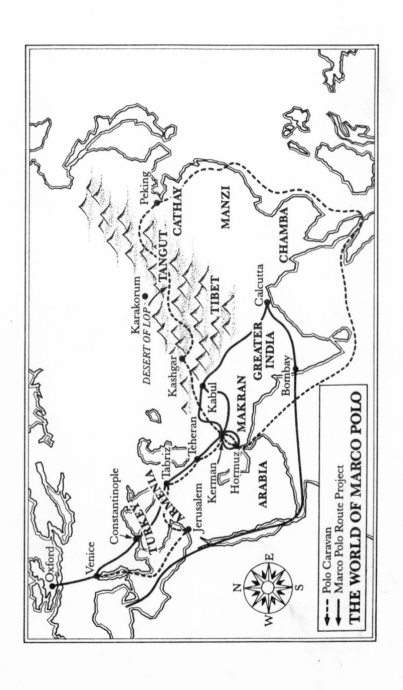

THE WORLD OF MARCO POLO

Oxford
Venice
Constantinople
TURKEY
ARMENIA
Jerusalem
Tabriz
Teheran
Kerman
Hormuz
ARABIA
Kabul
MAKRAN
Bombay
GREATER INDIA
Calcutta
CHAMBA
TIBET
Kashgar
DESERT OF LOP
Karakorum
TANGUT
CATHAY
MANZI
Peking

N
E
W
S

- - - Polo Caravan
——— Marco Polo Route Project

I

PREPARATIONS

Ye Emperors, Kings, Dukes, Marquises, Earls and Knights, and all the people desirous of knowing the diversities of the races of mankind, as well as the diversities of kingdoms, provinces and regions of all parts of the East, read through this book, and ye will find in it the greatest and most marvellous characteristics of the peoples, especially of Armenia, Persia, India and Tartary, as they are severally related in the present work by Marco Polo, a wise and learned citizen of Venice, who states distinctly what things he saw and what things he heard from others. For this book will be a truthful one. It must be known, then, that from the creation of Adam to the present day, no man, whether Pagan, or Saracen, or Christian, or other, of whatsoever progeny or generation he may have been, ever saw or inquired into so many and such great things as Marco Polo above mentioned.

SO BEGINS one of the world's most famous and fascinating books, originally published in the thirteenth century under the title of *A Description of the World* and now best known as *The Travels of Marco Polo*. The appeal of Marco Polo's tale seems to hold everlasting popularity, and for hundreds of years translations have been appearing in scores of languages ranging from Japanese to Irish.

In the fifteenth century the book's tales of Golden Cipango were read by Christopher Colombus, and the pages of one copy in the Biblioteca Colombia at Seville is marked with seventy notes, supposedly in the hand of the Great Admiral himself. In England, an Elizabethan edition by one John Frampton must have come into the hands of Frobisher, Drake and Raleigh. In the nineteenth century, a passage from Marco Polo's description of the summer palace of the Great Khan of the Mongols, inspired Coleridge to write his immortal line on the 'stately pleasure domes' of Xanadu, and even in the Jet Age one of the world's major airlines advertises that its planes fly a service along the Route of Marco Polo.

But more than anything else, the fascination of Marco Polo's book with its fabulous stories about the Great Roc and the gems of Golconda finds a special place in the imagination of young readers. The original book was written for the almost child-like imagination of the people of the Middle Ages, and today it still appeals most of all to a youthful public. For my own part I first read the story of Marco Polo's journey to mystic Cathay when I was at prep school, and can still remember the eagerness with which I followed his great journey and pictured myself travelling by caravan along the Old Silk Road eastward across all Asia to the canals and pagodas of China.

Ten years later while reading Geography at Oxford, it seemed slightly incongruous that Polo's name should come up in that section of the Honours School syllabus which is vaguely called the History of Geography. This time Polo's book was to be regarded as a reference for European knowledge of Asian geography in the thirteenth century. But academic interest in Marco Polo was only slight, for we were told that his book was too widely disbelieved in his own day to have much influence on his contemporaries and our attention was drawn rather to the works of the great Arab travellers, the Greek and Roman ideas on geography, and the arid histories of the development of obscure navigating instruments. But for me, that brief mention of Marco Polo had re-awakened my early fascination with his journey, and the rest of the course faded into the background. Luckily, the University Libraries provided me with all the material necessary for a quick survey of what was known about the great traveller.

In spite of Marco's world-wide fame, very few definite facts seemed to be known about Polo apart from a great deal of scholarly conjecture, mainly in the nineteenth century, on the

contents of the book itself. Most amazing of all, I could not find
that anyone had seriously tried to follow his route, and to compare the existing conditions with the country he described nearly
seven hundred years before. It was true that several parts of the
route had been covered at various times by different people, but
no single person with a geographer's training, however slight, had
attempted to follow the complete trail that wound across Turkey,
Persia, Afghanistan, over the Roof of the World and across China.
I decided that if it was possible, my boyhood dream of following
in the steps of Marco Polo would become reality.

At that time I had just started the second year of my three
year course at Oxford, and the obvious opportunity for the trip
was in the four months of the coming summer vacation in 1961.
Between June and September the deserts of Persia and Afghanistan would be at their hottest, and I had to find someone fool-
hardy enough to plan on crossing them with me. Surprisingly, I
found my companion within a week. Word got around my college
that I was planning a trip to China. Then someone mentioned that
he knew of another undergraduate, called Stanley Johnson, who
was toying with the same idea. On this vague piece of intelligence
I dropped into Exeter College one October afternoon and was
directed to Johnson's room. At my knock, a voice bellowed at me
to enter and I pushed in to find a burly young man with an unruly
shock of blond hair, sitting on the floor beside the wreckage of
his tea.

'Are you Johnson?' I asked.

'Yes,' the bear-like figure replied. So coming quickly to the
point I went on.

'My name's Tim Severin. I hear that you are thinking of going
to China next summer vac. Well, so am I, perhaps we could join
forces.'

'Splendid idea! Have some tea,' was the answer, and the Marco
Polo trip was under way.

Over that tea, we exchanged ideas. We found that we both held
Trevelyan Scholarships, and that both of us had at one time been
cowboys, Stan in Brazil and myself in Montana. Stan was determined to use his long summer holiday to continue his travels, and
was especially interested in seeing Asia. As an excuse to do this,
he was hoping to get permission to visit the Great Wall of China.

3

I explained my Marco Polo idea to him, and immediately his imagination grasped the attraction of the scheme and he was enthusiastic. By the time I returned to my own College for dinner, we had planned our opening moves. The two main essentials were money with which to finance ourselves, and permission to travel through the countries along Polo's route. But before we could get either, we had to formulate a more precise plan for our journey, so that we had a positive scheme to present to the various embassies and possible sponsors. Without this detailed plan we could not hope to obtain either visas or cash.

Since Stan was already deep in his preparations for University examinations at Easter, I disappeared back into the libraries for weeks of investigation into what field research we could usefully carry out on our trip, and also how we might best tackle the problems of travelling over the vast distances and difficult terrain. In the course of my studies, it became increasingly clear that by far the most genuine way of following Polo would be to take his book as our route guide and follow it, just like a guide book, from place to place. By doing this, we would be able to bridge the gap in time between the medieval traveller and ourselves, and as far as possible see the countryside as it now is, through his eyes. But to do this properly, it was vital that we should know as much as possible about the man we were following, so that we could understand his viewpoint and try to appreciate those things which had changed since his time or had remained unaltered for more than six centuries. One thing was certain, that despite the ages that separated us from Polo, the timelessness of the East and the factors that govern much of life there, terrain and climate, would be on our side, preserving living fragments of history.

In 1254 when Marco Polo was born, Europe was still deep in the Middle Ages. Dante was not yet known and Louis the Saint was King of France. Most of Europe was poor and only thinly populated. Italy was divided into city states which were continually squabbling amongst themselves. The two most powerful of these states, Genoa and Venice, were testing each other's strength for a final showdown. These two states were the most powerful not only in the Italian peninsula but in the Christian Mediterranean. To the East Crusader and Saracen disputed the Levant, whither the Crusaders were carried aboard Genoese or Venetian fleets which thereafter kept the life-line open (at a stiff profit). Every trading city from London to Baghdad had its twin colonies of Venetian and Genoese merchants.

But Europe and the forces of Islam paled into insignificance with the power that lay in the East. From the Arctic to the Himalayas, and from the White to the Yellow Seas, all the known world save the four peninsulas of India, Europe, Arabia and Indo-China, was ruled by the descendants of the Mongol Horde. Over that immense area it was said that 'not a dog might bark without Mongol leave'. Only fifty years earlier the stirring nucleus of Mongolia which was to explode across the face of the world, had thrown up its greatest warrior, Genghis Khan, Ocean Wide Lord, who having united the Mongols, decided, as Polo puts it, 'to conquer all the world'. Under Ogudai Khan, son and successor to Genghis, armies were sent out from the heart of the steppe Confederation at Karakorum, City of Black Walls. One expedition reached undefeated within a hundred miles of Berlin, another army struck south-west and overran Persia and Baghdad. No military force could check the savage onslaught of these hordes of mounted archers, whose courage, cruelty and mobility were legendary. In Europe the invaders first announced themselves by mangling the power of the dreaded Saracen. Then, just as Christendom was about to welcome the Mongols as allies against Islam, the Mongol armies pillaged the outlying Christian settlements with brutal ferocity. Christendom quailed at the shock, and hearing vague reports of a Mongol clan called Tatar Mongols, concluded that the terrifying nomads were indeed Tartars, sprung like Tartarus from the black demon legions of Hell.

To all points of the compass the Mongol armies roamed and conquered. But by 1260 their huge empire had grown so enormous that it began to split into separate kingdoms ruled by different branches of Genghis Khan's family, each branch paying lip service to the Khakhan or Overall Lord in the newly subdued Chinese territories. Even so, each of these subordinate Khanates was greater than any single European power, and within them the roads that led Eastward were kept open by Mongol law. Protected trade routes and rich oriental rulers eager for luxuries, these were golden opportunities which had not existed for adventurous traders since the time of Roman rule, and one of the first

5

parties to seize the chance and set out into the land of the Tartars on a commercial venture was, not surprisingly, a Venetian group, led by Nicolo and Maffeo Polo, the father and uncle of Marco, a young child left behind to grow up in Venice in the care of his aunt.

After many adventures the Venetians reached the Court of the Great Khan, and finding favour with him, were instructed to return to Europe in order to raise an Embassy from the Christian Courts to the Lord of All the Tartars. The return journey took the Polos three years, and the two brothers arrived home in Venice in 1269, to find that Nicolo's wife had died and his son, Marco, was fifteen years old and on the threshold of manhood by medieval standards.

For two years the brothers waited for a new Pope to be elected, as their home-coming had coincided with the Papal interregnum following the death of Pope Clement IV. Without Papal recognition the Polos dared not return to Peking, for the Khakhan, or Great Khan, Kublai, had strictly charged them that they should bring back to Peking 'a hundred men of learning, thoroughly acquainted with the principles of the Christian religion, well versed in the Seven Arts, and skilled to argue and demonstrate clearly to idolaters and those of other beliefs that their religion is utterly mistaken and that all the idols which they keep in their houses and worship are things of the devil—men able to show by clear reasoning that the Christian religion is better than theirs.' Furthermore the Great Khan directed the brothers to 'bring oil from the lamp that burns above the sepulchre of God in Jerusalem'.

It would need the Pope himself to authorize such an ambitious embassy from Rome to Peking, but despite the lavishness of the idea the Polos knew that such an expedition was feasible. For the Vatican was buzzing with rumours that somewhere to the East lay the fabled kingdom of Prester John, whose Christian armies would swoop down upon the rear of the Saracens and drive them out of the Holy Land for ever. All that Christendom needed to do was to locate Prester John and explain its plight.

Such was the background to the historic second journey of the Polo family, the journey which Marco Polo described so vividly in his book. It was easy for us to find many comparisons between his day and our own time. Once again most of Asia lay within one political bloc; we, the twentieth century travellers, were of much the same age and inclinations as Marco Polo himself: we too wanted to travel and observe. In the libraries I pieced together bit by bit the gaps in the academic knowledge about Polo's journey. Then at Christmas, armed with all the data, I went down to stay at Stan's farmhouse home on Exmoor. The winter snow kept us huddled over the fires, and by the end of a week we had hammered out our manifesto. In it we set out the objects of our trip and how much we thought it would cost to achieve. Then in the New Year we split forces and began the long round of charitable institutions and embassies. Following visits to London, Cambridge and our own Oxford Colleges we had soon amassed an impressive list of influential and eminent people who had listened kindly to our scheme. In particular Professor Needham gave us advice, and both Commander Courtney M.P. and the Far Eastern Department of the Foreign Office gave us all possible help in the realms of officialdom. But without exception they considered it extremely unlikely that we would ever obtain permission from the Chinese to cross their country.

Stan and I tried every approach that we could think of to persuade the Chinese authorities to produce visas for us. We sent circulars to the various departments in Peking; we made plans to take a Chinese student with us; and we stressed that as students we were strictly non-political. The Chinese Embassy in Portland Square became the target for numerous visits and telephone calls. But all to no avail; visas were not forthcoming. This, however, was not altogether unexpected and we directed our energies elsewhere. Our visas for Yugoslavia, Bulgaria and Persia were easily obtained and only Afghanistan remained a problem. Eventually permission came through from Kabul, and one March afternoon we drove jubilantly down from Oxford to collect our passports from the Embassy. Stan picked me up from my college, Keble, in an ancient car. Also with us was a Russian Exchange Student who wanted a lift into London. It was the first time that I had driven with Stan, and the whole experience proved rather unnerving. Between Oxford and Hyde Park Corner, Stan was involved in no less than three minor collisions, and at the fourth disaster our Russian passenger fled looking very shaken. Then on the final run-in to the Afghan Embassy Stan failed to notice the frantic signals of a traffic policeman, who busily made a note of the car's registration number. Accordingly while I dropped off for the passports, Stan drove on to the nearest scrap dealer where he sold his jalopy for the price of our rail fare back to Oxford.

By this time our respective tutors were seeing less and less of their pupils, and it became clear that we had to expand the Marco Polo organization. The new member of our group was my elder brother, Brian, who had recently gone down from Oxford and started with the Publicity Section of Richard Costain & Company, a large construction firm. Despite the difficulties of his new job, Brian plunged into the trials and tribulations of being our Home Agent. Based in London, he was in a position to help us enormously, and that, in part, overcame our sense of isolation at Oxford. By the end of our trip, Brian was to have played a major part in the success of our venture. While the Home Agent cannot share the excitement and adventure of the luckier travellers, the people in the field depend almost entirely on his resourcefulness and efficiency to see their project through to a successful conclusion. Certainly, with respect to the Marco Polo trip, our planning was so sketchy and rudimentary that we left behind many problems which we did not have time to consider and which Brian had to manage once we were gone. Not the least of these unsolved dilemmas was the fact that our itinerary comprised three and a half months of Easterly travelling, leaving just two weeks in which to get back to Oxford for the new term. The rub was that we had no idea whatsoever where we would be at the end of our three and a half months, and still less idea of how we would get back to England. Our Home Agent had the task of arranging this when the time came, bearing in mind that whatever the solution, it must not cost any money for we had no finances to spare for our trip home.

Side by side with our efforts to get visas from the countries concerned, we went the round of the societies and organizations which in the past had financed University expeditions. Immediately we found ourselves in difficulties, for we had placed high hopes on receiving grants from some of them. But the learned bodies could not envisage that we would ever succeed in crossing the appalling terrain that we would encounter along Polo's trail. They felt that the jeeps which we intended to use were not as flexible or durable as the mules, camels and horses which had made up the Polo caravans. The expedition selection committees threw up their hands in horror at our methods of preparation. They could not conceive that a trip could possibly leave England within six months of the preliminary idea being put forward. We were told that not only would we fail to find anything interesting or worthwhile about Polo, but our tiny group would perish in the deserts due to a criminal absence of any attention to essential details and the minutiae of expedition preparation. It was no use replying that Marco Polo had managed the trip with tremendous success but without any of the paraphernalia of modern planning which were so strenuously advocated. The Marco Polo Route Project was granted neither recognition nor cash, and so we decided that our scheme would stand or fall by our own efforts to finance and carry it through.

As a first drastic step we decided to discount any hope of getting into China and concentrate on covering the ancient caravan track as far as the High Pamirs. Indeed, this part of Polo's route held the richest potential for our research into the Venetian's descriptions of his travels. Secondly, we struck out into an entirely new line in expedition transport. To date, the standard vehicle had always been the Land-Rover or army lorry. We could halve our costs by travelling not on four wheels but on two and resolved that we would use motorcycles. We took this decision not only from the financial point of view, but also because we felt that motorcycles could be taken along trails too narrow for bigger vehicles, and we did not know into what straits our journeying would take us. Above all this decision in favour of motorcycles was an outright challenge to all those people who said that we would never manage it. There was no denying that we were exposing ourselves to enormous difficulties. Motorcycles were untried and might prove too fragile for the heavy demands we would make upon them. Alternatively we might easily injure ourselves in handling them over rough country, or become so exhausted that we could not continue our trip. Despite all these gloomy predictions Stan and I pushed ahead with the idea, which made most people regard us as determined suicides.

Two months before we were due to set out, we had persuaded the B.S.A Company to loan to us for the trip one of their big twin-cylinder Shooting Star machines. An identical companion machine was presented to us by my brother's firm, Richard Costain, who regarded the whole project with detached amusement and with the generosity to appreciate the originality of such a far-fetched scheme. Stan and I then dashed up to Birmingham for a flying visit to the motorcycle factory, so that we might have a chance of learning a little about the motorcycle engines. But the professional mechanics talked in riddles as far as we laymen were concerned, so we gave up and returned to Oxford to await delivery of the motorcycles.

Suddenly our financial position improved. Keble College gave me a generous grant, and we managed to sell the newspaper and book rights of our forthcoming trip. A Marco Polo account was opened and we obtained two sidecars, one shaped like a coffin for our stores and the other a more normal passenger version.

All this time there was one point which we had not dared to make public; the fact that neither Stan nor I knew anything at all about motorcycles. Indeed, neither of us had ever held a motorcycle licence, and we both supposed that as a form of transport motorbikes were a dirty, noisy and smelly proposition. However, we had to keep silent about this, for sponsors, not unnaturally, would fade away overnight if they found out that we were proposing to set out across unknown trails in Asia without ever having straddled a motorcycle before. The least we could do was to obtain a motorcycle driving licence, and so the two of us applied for a test in Oxford. Despite the fact that the Driving Test was conducted in the road that surrounds my own College, the Ministry examiner had no hesitation in pronouncing that both Stan and I after our performance on a borrowed motor scooter, were totally unfit to drive on English roads. Sadly we agreed with him.

By this time our projected trip was receiving a certain amount of newspaper publicity, and it became known that we were on the look-out for a cameraman for the Marco Polo team. Among the letters which we received from eager volunteers was one signed 'Michael de Larrabeiti'. The name misled us into thinking that the writer would be a rather delicate individual unsuited to the roughriding that lay ahead. Nevertheless we invited him up to Oxford for an interview. Our visitor turned out to be about ten years older than us, a wiry, bespectacled, balding Londoner with a cockney's wit and a deep-rooted wanderlust. In a few moments we knew that our cameraman had been found, for Mike was not only experienced in film work, having been a professional camera-man, but had wandered the world on his own account. That first evening when he found that he had missed the last train to London, he casually swallowed a meal of raw eggs from their shells and turned in to sleep for five hours, stretched out on the floor of my study, before catching the milk train back to his day's work with a film company. Most impressive of all, he did not even falter when we explained that he had just one week in which to have all the necessary inoculations and find a film company who would be willing to provide cameras and films for our journey. The night before our departure he was back in Oxford with all this accom-plished.

Inevitably that last week was a hectic rush for everyone concerned with the trip. B.S.A. were unable to deliver our machines until the last minute, so in the meantime we fitted our-selves out in smart motorcyclist's clothing with black uniforms and tall black jackboots. Our helmets were painted light blue and in the front appeared the letters M.P.R.P. which stood for the Marco Polo Route Project. This flamboyance was not without reason, for all of us were sufficiently experienced in this sort of travel to know that in many situations a semi-military appearance can work wonders with minor officialdom, and in any event motor-cycle clothing is specially designed for heavy use. The long boots we chose proved in the end to be a very wise selection. Not only did they stand up to the heaviest wear under the most exacting condi-tions, but they also protected our feet and legs from injury, giving valuable ankle support whenever we had to put our feet on the ground to stop the motorcycles falling over. Mike was particularly pleased with his heavy boots and crash helmet, as he lovingly ex-plained that the use of head and feet are particularly effective in bar-room brawls.

The question whether we should take firearms never really concerned us, for we felt that guns were likely to prove more of a liability than an asset. We would not be in a position to hunt for the pot, largely because of the barren country, and in the wilder parts of Turkey, Persia and Afghanistan any guns we had with us would be a tempting prize for thugs. Indeed, we took so little with us that we had almost nothing worth stealing, for it was a basic principle of the Marco Polo Route Project that, like Polo himself, we would attempt to live off the land as much as possible in the manner of the local people. By the very nature of our theme we had no heavy scientific instruments to weigh us down and no precise research routine to restrain us. Our vehicles did not isolate us from our surroundings nor did we wish it. In all this we differed greatly from the average Land-Rover party driving loftily eastward, carrying food, medical supplies, spare clothing, camp beds, blankets and so forth. Our carrying capacity was so limited that we brusquely limited ourselves to a sleeping bag each, one small tent, iron rations, a tiny stove, the tools and a few spare parts for the motorcycles, and the camera equipment. No spare clothes were allowed, and we rationed ourselves to one handkerchief per head ! The result of all this was that we were a small, highly mobile group living much closer to the local conditions than our detached luxurious cousins on four wheels who even found time to boil their drinking water.

The last four days before departure were spent working on the motorcycles. The manufacturers had very kindly carried out most of the modifications which we had suggested. Very strong rear shock-absorbers had been fitted and also low gear ratios because of the severe loading we were forced to impose. Low compression pistons and special sparking plugs were intended to overcome the problems of poor grade petrol which we were almost sure to encounter nearly everywhere beyond Yugoslavia and to which our sophisticated machines were totally unsuited, for the motorcycles were designed for high-speed travelling along smooth tarmac roads. To carry spare petrol as well as our drinking water, we took excellent lightweight jerricans made from polythene, and on the outside of the passenger sidecar we slung the specially studded cross-country tyres, so that they would act as fender until we were better motorcyclists. The inside of the passenger sidecar where Mike was scheduled to ride, I stuffed with foam rubber padding to reduce buffeting, and under his seat we fashioned a small concealed compartment to hold the cameras which might be subject to confiscation.

All this preliminary work was carried out in Temple's Garage in Oxford. Mr. Temple himself gave us the benefit of his broad experience. Once he had tuned motorcycles for Lawrence of Arabia, and now he bustled around offering useful suggestions while his mechanics swarmed over the machines. Typical of his more unorthodox and rewarding ideas was that we could overcome the problem of keeping sand out of the engines by stretching ladies nylon stockings over the carburettor air intakes.

Our official departure had been timed for the afternoon of June 21st, and before we set off we invited all those who had helped us to a farewell party in the quadrangle of Exeter College. Resplendent in our expedition uniforms amid the marquees of the previous evening's Summer Ball, we toasted the success of the trip. The cameras whirred, the motorcycles roared into activity and we swung out of the great front porch of the College, apparently off for 10,000 miles across all Asia, but in fact straight back to Temple's Garage where we put in another six hours of hard work on our motorcycles.

Our real departure next morning was a much more sombre affair. This time the machines were loaded beyond recognition and the rain dripped steadily down from a leaden sky. Only Mike in his new jackboots saved the day with a spontaneous and hilarious imitation of a Nazi stormtrooper. Our final motto was no gloriously flamboyant slogan but a muttered reminder that at all costs we must avoid English policemen for it would be a little damping if the Marco Polo Route Project ground to a halt on English roads because we still had no motorcycle driving licences.

After a few bungled attempts Stan and I coaxed our respective machines into life, and very gingerly we set out towards London. At first we could not exceed even a bare 35 m.p.h. for the motorcycles were not yet run in, and we found that changing gear at the same time as steering the outfits was a nerve-wracking performance. Anyone following the Marco Polo Route Project along the A40 would have seen the two machines describing a series of wobbly arcs as they weaved along the road. We had to learn for ourselves that in order to go in a straight line on a motorcycle that is dragging along a heavily loaded sidecar, one has to achieve a delicate balance between throttle and steering. For when one loses speed on the bike, the sidecar travels on with its own momentum, pushing the motorcycle to the right and into the on-coming traffic. Alternatively, when the rider of the motorcycle tries to compensate for this by opening the throttle, he finds himself out-accelerating the sidecar and finishes up by pirouetting around it to the alarm of his passenger, in this case Mike, who found himself at one moment in the middle of the road and at the next instant scraping along the kerb.

One of the earliest of our decisions was that each member of the team would be responsible for a particular aspect of expedition routine. Thus Stan was to keep the logbook, Mike was in charge of all photography, and my own responsibility included the academic side of the trip as well as the role of expedition mechanic. It was therefore with my heart in my mouth that I listened to the engine note from our over-loaded, untried machines as they chugged along those first few miles. The most immediate worry was the woeful sluggishness of the motorcycles, as they did not seem nearly as fiery and powerful as I had expected. This certainly did not augur well for the heavy churning grind that we would expect in sandy regions, but it was far too late to do anything about it at that stage. We pressed on to London, stopping off only to buy two sets of 'heavy-duty' motorcycle panniers for our machines which had even less luggage space than we imagined. Then we drove down to the Ferryfield at Lydd, where we supervised the loading of our precious vehicles on to the cross-channel aircraft.

As we walked across the concrete to the waiting plane, I could not help feeling pleased that if we had done nothing else, we had at least confounded the pundits who had predicted that the Marco Polo Route Project would never even leave England.

2

TO VENICE

AFTER A BRIEF FLIGHT across the Channel, our air ferry
touched down at Le Touquet Airport and disgorged its passengers
into the airport transit building. There we were unpleasantly surprised to find that during the hasty last-minute packing we had
apparently left behind a vital folder containing most of our documents, including the papers for the motorcycles and £40 worth
of petrol vouchers. The irony of the situation was that now we
were in France, both Stan and I could legitimately drive the motorcycles, for our International Driving Permits issued on the
strength of English motorcar licences covered the use of motorcycles. The French Customs officers were understandably bewildered that we, who hoped to cross Asia, were so inept as to
forget the simple documents necessary to cross France. But in the
end they let us proceed once we had bought an Insurance Certificate, and then inevitably, as we packed up to leave, the truant
folder was discovered tucked away in the nose of Mike's sidecar.
It was a lesson worth remembering, that with even the limited
capacity available on our machines, it was still possible to mislay
equipment and papers, and we could not afford to let it happen
later on.

With our high spirits considerably chastened by this experience,
we drove out of the airport, and in doing so, very nearly succeeded
in running down a small, middle-aged Frenchman complete with
shabby raincoat and beret, who ran out in front of our machines,

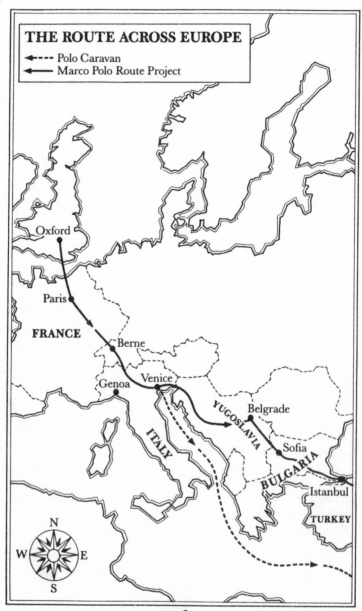

THE ROUTE ACROSS EUROPE

◄---- Polo Caravan
◄──── Marco Polo Route Project

Oxford

Paris

FRANCE

Berne

Genoa

Venice

ITALY

YUGOSLAVIA

Belgrade

Sofia

BULGARIA

Istanbul

TURKEY

N
W E
S

16

excitedly waving his arms. It turned out that he was a reporter from the local newspaper, the Voix du Nord, and had been sent out by his editor to get a story about the three young Englishmen who were setting off to follow the route of Marco Polo. He opened his interview in atrocious English and was obviously very relieved when all three of us answered simultaneously in French. But it was Mike who really excelled himself, for he had lived some time in France, and is a confirmed Francophile. Thus while our reporter friend was interested to learn that Stan and I had been cowboys, he was in rhapsodies when he found out that Mike had once been a mountain shepherd in Provence and had walked the long trail of the transhumance with the flocks on their way to summer pastures in the Alps. So while Stan and I fretted to be off on our way to Paris, Mike and the caricature of a Frenchman rattled away at each other with such effect that next morning the Voix du Nord carried a lyrical article all about 'le Berger de Provence, casqué de bleu comme le ciel de chez nous'.

We had hardly left our newspaper man when one of the motor-cycles ran out of petrol, so that we ended up by spending the first night of the expedition on the sand-dunes outside Le Touquet. In so doing, we managed to get more sand in our sleeping bags than we ever collected in them subsequently across the deserts of Persia and Afghanistan. Next morning we chugged on to Paris, gradually becoming more proficient at driving our machines, though they still seemed unhappily sluggish.

It was during this drive that Stan and I began to appreciate the difficulties of making a film about our trip. Mike had to be cameraman and film editor at the same time. He had to visualize the various scenes as they would eventually fit together in the final film, and then photograph the different, and often widely separated, sequences in the most interesting manner possible. For this, his equipment of two ancient 16 mm. cameras was pitifully meagre by film company standards, but he made up for it with a persuasive tongue. Time after time he would prevail upon Stan and me to stop, while he set up his tripod and sent us back down the road we had come. Then at his signal the two machines would come sweeping back past him as he crouched over his whirring camera.

Naturally the best way of depicting our arrival in Paris would be to film the motorcycles roaring around the Arc de Triomphe.

To Venice

Unfortunately it was late afternoon by the time we reached the city and the rush-hour traffic was in full cry. But Mike calmly erected his apparatus in the middle of the road and at considerable risk to life and limb filmed Stan and me as we drove our way through the mass of milling vehicles. Not surprisingly, this sort of activity rapidly attracted the attention of the police, and we were descended upon by no less a force than a patrol of the motorized Garde Mobile resplendent in their white breeches, scarlet facings, gleaming crash helmets and immaculate white gloves. Fortunately any atmosphere of stern police reprimands vanished when our interrogators noticed the B.S.A. Shooting Stars. Led by their Sergeant, the patrol clustered eagerly around our machines examining every detail, as the model we were riding was not yet available in France, and soon a voluble discussion arose on the comparative merits of the B.S.A. and other makes of motorcycle, with the final verdict that for high-speed work on the open road, 'la belle B.S.A. c'est vraiment nerveux'.

As we could not afford a hotel room, Mike and I surreptitiously slept the night on the grass of the Bois de Bolougne whilst Stan stayed with friends. Then in the morning, we took the machines to a garage to have the oil changed, now that we had partly run-in the engines. Whilst this was being done, I took the opportunity of mentioning the noticeable lack of power to the senior mechanic in the garage. With the air of one having to deal with a fool, and especially a person who was maltreating a powerful road-racing bike, he unscrewed the air filter, tore out the offending heavy-duty gauze filling and threw it expressively into a far corner. The improvement in performance was astounding, and it was with much lighter hearts that we put Paris behind us and struck south-east for Switzerland and ultimately Venice.

The new-found power in the motorcycles rather went to Stan's head, and soon he was outpacing me on the heavier vehicle that was pulling the stores sidecar. In the other sidecar Mike could not help observing that Stan seemed to be very slow in noticing other road-users or bends in the road. When taxed with this at a tea halt, Stan rather sheepishly informed us that he had lost his driving glasses just before leaving England. But as somebody else had left their own pair of glasses in his room, he had brought those along, 'as they would be just as good'.

Another difficulty now reared its head, for our sidecars had been fitted on the left-hand side of the motorcycles. This was excellent for English roads, but for driving on the right in Europe it was a distinctly alarming arrangement. With the increased speed available, Stan was now passing very nearly every other machine on the road. Unfortunately, on each occasion his vision would be obscured by the vehicle ahead so that he would edge over into the middle of the road in an attempt to see round it. When this happened, poor Mike helplessly cooped up in the sidecar, would get a terrifying first view of any approaching danger, and even when Stan had been forced back into line, he had a habit of leaving Mike projecting into the stream of oncoming traffic. It was useless for Mike to shout a warning, as his driver could not hear above the rush of the slipstream and the roar of the engine. So in the end I had the entertaining sight, as I followed the happy couple, of Stan steadily sidling his machine out into the middle of the road until Mike's wiry arm shot up out of the sidecar clutching a rolled-up newspaper, with which he belaboured Stan over the head, not stopping until Stan had resumed station.

In this erratic manner we had a splendid run across France in glorious weather, and crossed into Switzerland, where the Turkish Ambassador in Berne was a distant relative of Stan's family and had very generously invited the expedition to call on him. But the roads leading in to Berne were packed with long queues of cars, as Sunday afternoon trippers returned to their city. So after bowling merrily along the Routes Nationales of Franche Comté, we found ourselves inexorably wedged in the long slow-moving lines of stolid Swiss burghers who were in no hurry to get home, whereas we had promised to see our Turkish host for dinner. Trying to gain time in the crowd of vehicles was very like hoping to get away early from Twickenham just after an International match; at every minor cross-roads the queues halted while more traffic filtered in. We were getting desperate, when Mike had a characteristic inspiration. Leaping out of his sidecar, he stalked imperiously up the line of vehicles. Then at the bottle-neck itself, his black-uniformed and jackbooted figure halted, turned, and with the manner born, held up the traffic with one hand and with the other waved on the Marco Polo Route Project. Stan and I swung the motorcycles out of the queue and straight-faced beneath our blue helmets, drove past the long line of patient law-abiding motorists until we reached Mike. Equally straight-faced, he stepped smartly into his sidecar and we accelerated away for a repeat performance at the next traffic hold-up. In this way we managed to reach the Turkish Embassy just in time, and after an excellent dinner were put up for the night. Next morning a pot of orange paint was produced, and the motorcycle panniers were daubed with the optimistic words

OXFORD—VENICE—CHINA

Our journey was already behind the original optimistic schedule, so having thanked our hosts we said goodbye regretfully and pressed on towards Italy.

Mike (as he was not occupied with driving) was promoted to the job of navigator, and under his direction we looped our way along the Alpine roads in the direction of the St. Gothard Pass. The roads were peculiarly empty and soon we were climbing up into the mountains themselves, where the scenery became more impressive with, at one point, the splendid blue-green opalescence of a glacier. Our labouring machines were making poor going of the climb, and as the afternoon changed to evening it was obvious that the main ridge had yet to be crossed. Mike however, assured us that the St. Gothard lay just ahead and so we persevered, comforting ourselves with the thought that the conditions were providing a preliminary test for our untried, heavily loaded machines. Gradually the road deteriorated into patches of snow, melt-water and outwash debris. Stubbornly we coaxed the motorcycles in bottom gear around ever-sharpening hairpin bends, and by nightfall we had crossed the highest point with great difficulty. Dropping down in the dark to a small village on the other side, we stopped for supper and found out that we had crossed, not the St. Gothard, but the Furka Pass. The villagers were astounded and so were we. The Furka Pass (one of the most gruelling passes in Switzerland) was officially closed at that time of year, and we had actually covered much of the descent by the gleam of our side-lights. By an expedition vote of 2-1 Mike was asked to surrender custody of the Route Project's maps.

Reluctantly we decided that, as we were so far behind schedule, we would have to push on through the night. The decision was a bad one, for it began to rain heavily and soon the road became very slippery. As we snaked our way down the Ticino valley, Stan pulled steadily ahead only to meet with disaster. A sudden S-bend sent his machine out of control and it spun crazily into a stone wall. Luckily neither Mike nor Stan were injured, but as I came round the corner, my own motorcycle's headlight shewed the other machine on one side of the road, while on the opposite verge lay its wheel-less sidecar with Mike still sitting in it, like a chick half broken from its shell. Stoically we pitched the tent near the scene of the crash and awaited daylight. With great restraint Mike mentioned to Stan that perhaps he could drive a shade more cautiously in future.

'Oh! Come off it,' Stan exclaimed.

'We did, mate! We did,' was the instant rejoinder.

As a result of the crash, I spent two days of hard work in the local blacksmith's shop mending the damage, while my companions made friends with the small children of the village. From them they learnt that 'Salta Gigino, Salta Gigetto!' is the Italian version of Two Little Dicky Birds, and that if one spells B.S.A. forwards and backwards it reads 'Bisogne Sapere Andere Anche Senza Benzina' (it is necessary to know how to go without petrol). But despite my efforts, or maybe because of them, the unfortunate passenger sidecar never really recovered. Thenceforth it drooped like a tired wing, its wheel wobbling and fluttering to such an extent that Mike expected to part company with his driver at any moment, and it was in this lop-sided condition we eventually reached Venice.

Of the days of Venetian glory when Marco Polo had walked among bustling, prosperous throngs on the Piazza San Marco, the poet has written :—

What, they lived once thus at Venice, where the merchants
were the kings.
Where St. Mark's is, where the Doges used to wed the sea with
rings.*

But like Tyre, these days are long since gone, for it seemed that the only merchant princes of our time are the couriers from the

*Robert Browning, *A Toccata of Galuppi's.*

tourist agencies. As a boy Marco Polo would have mingled on the waterfront with traders brought there on business from as far afield as Russia and Ethiopia. Now the great square of San Marco bustles with Japanese, Americans, West Germans and Scandinavians. Many are men of business, but they come there not for trade, but to stand and stare. Modern Venice seems more like an enormous fairground, a superficiality of hotels and glossy advertisements, which can hardly compare with the carnivals once held on the more solid basis of her medieval commercial prowess. Four years before he set forth on his great journey, Marco must have seen the great guild pageant given under the order of Doge Lorenzo Tiepolo. For fully half a day the splendid procession flowed past, shipbuilders, glass workers, leatherworkers and goldsmiths. Every guild was represented by the symbols of its craft, and each Court of Elders was majestically rowed past by companies of richly liveried retainers, all this in honour of Venice, La Serenissima.

Marco Polo was born to a senior family of Venice, which traced its lineage back to eleventh century settlers from Dalmatia. Like the other leading families of Venice, the Polos derived and exercised their position through trade. In Venice, Constantinople, and even at Soldaia in the far Crimea, the three starlings of the Polo crest appeared above warehouses and trading offices. Venice was Queen of the Seas, and at the vast Arsenal slave labour turned out the fleets that made it possible. Pride of the city, this great Arsenal was a town in itself, capable of building a hundred ships in a hundred days or impressing Henry III of France with a demonstration of the feverish shipyard drill which in rather more than two hours turned a hulk on the shipways into a fully equipped war galley beating out to sea. The Adriatic was no more than a Venetian lake ruled by Venetian flotillas. At the oars served specially trained Dalmatian freemen, and in proud command of each vessel sailed a gentleman-commander from the merchant family that had donated the sleek warship to Venice, La Serenissima.

But by the mid-thirteenth century Genoa's growing sea power challenged Venice's rule of the waves, and the two city-states clashed in the struggle for maritime supremacy. By a strange stroke of fate, it was this rivalry between Venice and Genoa which saved Marco Polo's noble journey from sinking into obscurity. As it so

happened, when Marco returned from his travels, he captained a
Venetian warship and was taken prisoner by the Genoese during
a sea-battle, reputedly while putting up a gallant rear-guard action
at the Battle of Curzola. The Genoese admiral had sworn 'to bit
the horses of San Marc's', and the captured galleys were ignomini-
ously towed stern-first into Genoa's harbour, their proud pennants
trailing in the water. Then, for three years Marco was held
prisoner with other captives in the Palazzo di San Giorgio, until
on May 25th 1299 an exchange of prisoners was negotiated under
an armistice arranged by Matteo Visconti, Captain-General of
Milan.

During those years of captivity the word soon spread throughout Genoa that in the cells was a man who had ventured far into
the mysterious East. According to this Venetian captive, the
Orient was not a vast, wailing bog inhabited by man-eating hob-
goblins, but a wondrous Paradise where there rose great cities
twelve times greater than Genoa or Venice. Marco was besieged
by people who wanted to hear more of his amazing stories, and
the description of his wanderings was immensely popular. Fortunately one of Marco's fellow-prisoners was a professional story-
teller and romancer, one Rustichello of Pisa, whose own city-state
had been crushed by the Genoese. In order to save himself the
weary repetition of his more popular stories, Marco was persuaded
to collaborate with the professional story-teller and produce a
book. Permission was given for Marco to send to his father
in Venice for the notes that he had made on the trip. Then with
the help of these and his own phenomenal memory, a typical
medieval characteristic, the great book was compiled.

By 1298 it was finished and immediately became popular,
though not as a factual account of the world, but rather as a work
of fiction, a collection of mythical descriptions. Partly this was the
fault of the romantic way in which Rustichello set out the tale, but
mainly because the European mind was too limited at that time
to grasp Marco Polo's astounding revelations. Until Marco returned from the land of the Tartars, the merchants of the eastward trade routes had deliberately exaggerated and falsified the
fables and legends about the East, for this not only put up the
price of the Oriental goods that they had for sale, but also discouraged competitors. Then Marco Polo came back home, like a

new Ulysses to Ithaca, with tales of a civilized people who used money made from paper and who burned black rocks so that they kept warm in the winter. According to this Polo, asbestos was not the skin of the fiery salamander, but was dug from the ground like a stone. Such tales were hard to believe and the public scoffed that the poor fellow must have gone mad with the torment of his wanderings. Marco soon acquired the reputation of a champion liar and was dubbed 'Il Milione', for he was the man who bragged in terms of hundreds of thousands. Such tales were entertaining, but not nearly so credible as those of the purely fictitious Sir John Mandeville, for this mythical traveller was careful to recount sights that the bigoted European audience could easily imagine. Indeed Marco was so far ahead of his time that it was not until the end of the nineteenth century that some parts of his route was re-visited and modern travellers testified to the truth of his descriptions.

Even today it comes as a surprise that in Venice most people still refer to Marco Polo not by his name, but as 'Il Milione', and his legends still flicker in the modern tourist town. Time and again we were told that somewhere in the Corte del Milione, where once stood the Polo house, is buried a fabulous treasure, a great coffer filled with the precious stones he brought back from Cathay. Astonishingly, even people who should have known better thought that the story of Marco Polo was a fairy tale, and his book no more than a subtle invention. Perhaps this modern scepticism has its roots far back in the days when in Marco's own life-time people regarded his stories as creations of his imagination. But at least we hoped our own trip would help reduce this discredit and bring a little more justice to the great traveller.

Another aspect of this absence of real recognition for Polo is that, although in many ways Marco Polo was the greatest son of Venice, his own birthplace forgot him and is only belatedly making up for this error. Before we left Oxford we wrote to the Mayor of Venice to tell him of our impending trip. In due course we received a letter back, addressed to Signore Johnson and Severin. In it, His Excellency Faveretto Fabrici graciously invited us to call upon him in the Doge's Palace when we reached his city. Accordingly when we arrived in Venice, one of the first things we did was to arrange an interview with the Mayor for the next day.

But some spark of mischief tempted us to tilt at the windmill. We decided that for the honour of poor neglected Marco Polo we would make our appearance before the Mayor with as much flourish as possible.

With this in mind we laid plans to produce our motorcycles in the Piazza San Marco, which is forbidden to traffic and surrounded by canals. It fell on Stan to scout forward and arrange water transport. Unfortunately a linguistic muddle between Stan and a very furtive gondolier led the latter to think that he was being engaged to ferry two small motor-assisted bicycles to St. Marks. Then, at the appointed hour the Marco Polo Route Project drove down to the wharf only to find that the hired craft was a mere cockleshell which would sink like a stone beneath our cumbersome machines. Our waterman accomplice was therefore despatched to find a larger boat. But we had lost the element of surprise and had been spotted by the 'Polizia'. Policemen of every description descended upon us, Naval Police, Traffic Police and even Tourist Police. We remonstrated with them, hoping against hope that our boatman would reappear. But very sensibly he had decamped for good, and eventually there arrived on the scene no less a personage than Il Colonnello di Carabineri himself. He examined our letter from the Mayor, telephoned the Mayor's Secretary and escorted us to a police launch. Thus it was that under open arrest and without our motorcycles we went for our interview with Il Sindaco di Venezia.

The whole performance was short and sweet. The Mayor greeted us on behalf of the city and presented us with a beautifully illustrated copy of Marco Polo's book. In halting Italian Stan replied, and we toasted the success of the expedition. Then as we left, the Mayor's aide pressed a voucher for 100 litres of petrol into my hand. Venice, it seemed, was still invincible, and the members of the expedition were silently amused that the official reaction of Marco Polo's native city to our visit was to give us the wherewithal to speed our departure from its boundaries. In fairness to the Mayor, however, he was a very busy man, especially in the tourist season, and we appreciated the fact that he had found time to see us at all.

Next we turned our attention to filming what we could of Marco Polo's Venice. On the surface the city has changed little.

To Venice

Lagoons, gondolas and canals are much the same now as then. But it is difficult to feel that a city which depends upon injections of concrete to hold it above water is La Serenissima, where in times of siege the defenders once fired derisive cannonballs of bread at their besiegers. In those days Venice held sway over part of the Lombard Plain, the Dalmatian coast, many Greek islands and numerous enclaves in Asia Minor. The Doge bore the strange, but proud, title of 'Lord of a Half and a Quarter of the Roman Empire' and each year the city was wedded to the sea at the ceremony of La Sensa. Venetian fleets ruled the Black Sea, the Agean Sea and the Sea of Marmora. Trade and more trade were her ambitions. Venetian mirrors of polished steel formed part of the finest dowries in Persia. Every year a fleet sailed to England with spices, and returned loaded with wool.

Her trade in silk, spices and gems provided the glamour of Venetian merchant venturing but this was delicate traffic, easily upset in times of trouble. In the long run the flourishing fortunes of the great merchant princes were based on the main staples of commerce, iron, salt, wood, furs and slaves. The more risky luxury trade was left to men like the Polo brothers, who handled high-value goods like silk, because it stood the economic demands of long journeys, or precious stones, which could easily be concealed when caravans were attacked.

One of the most famous legends of all concerning the Polos recounts how Marco, with his father Nicolo and uncle Maffeo, returned to Venice after twenty-four years of wandering. The three adventurers went immediately to the Ca'Polo and there discovered that cousins had moved into the family home during their absence. As no news had been heard from the Polos for many years, the three men had been given up for dead and now it was difficult for them to establish their identity, as they wore Mongol clothes and talking in halting Venetian, using many outlandish phrases. But, after bribing the gate-keeper the three travellers were allowed to enter, and their more immediate relatives decided that the newcomers were in fact the long-lost merchant venturers. The travellers came unescorted and their clothes were drab and travel-stained. And so, the legend goes on, they were taken in temporarily and given a change of clothing. But when Uncle Maffeo found out that his wife had given away his

26

travelling clothes to a beggar, he flew into a great rage, and borrowing a spinning wheel rushed off with it to St. Mark's Square.

In the Piazza he set up the spinning wheel and began to turn it without using any wool. For three days he sat there while the crowds stood and stared curiously at a man spinning vacantly to no purpose. The idling wits strolled over from the gaming tables near the water's edge and passed facetious remarks about the poor simpleton whose trip eastward had addled his brains. But Maffeo said nothing and spurned the entreaties of his family who begged him to return home. On the third day the beggar who wore Maffeo's old clothes joined the crowd that mocked and jeered, then Maffeo leapt to his feet and seizing the beggar, offered to exchange clothes a second time. This was too much for the bystanders, who dissolved into mirth at such idiocy, and the story became a nine days wonder throughout the city.

A few days later, every noble family in Venice received invitations to the Ca'polo for a huge banquet to welcome home the three Polos. Curious and eager for further diversion, the guests gathered in the great hall. The arrangements were impeccable; tables, servants, food and wine were excellent. Then as the assembled company sat down for the meal, the three hosts appeared at the head of the table, dressed in splendid robes of crimson satin. At the end of the first course, the Polos withdrew and then returned a few moments later clad in even more gorgeous robes of crimson damask. The first set of robes were cut up and distributed among the servants. This amazed the guests, for in the Middle Ages one of the very few ways of shewing off one's wealth was to wear costly clothing. Twice more the incredible happened, as the Polos changed from crimson damask to crimson velvet and then to cloth of gold. At their final appearance, the chronicler concludes, the three hosts carried in their coarse and ragged travelling garments. Then, holding them aloft, they took sharp knives with which they slit open the seams and pleats :—

> to bring from them enormous quantities of the most precious gems such as rubies, sapphires, carbuncles, diamonds and emeralds which had been sewn up in the said garments with such cunning and in such a fashion that none would have been able to imagine that they were there. For when they took their

departure from the Great Khan, they changed all the gold which he had given them into so many rubies, emeralds and other precious stones, knowing well that had they done otherwise it would never have been possible for them to carry so much gold with them over such a long, difficult and far-reaching road.

In fact the chronicler did not know that in China at that time the use of gold was an Imperial monopoly. But, at any rate, such profusion of wealth was sufficient proof for the merchant families to credit the claim of the three travellers to the name of Polo.

All that remains of the house where these events are supposed to have taken place is a double-arched doorway in the northwest corner of the Corte del Milione. It is a sad area at the junction of the Rio San Giovanni Grisostomo and the Rio San Marino, two minor canals along which the tourist gondolas seldom venture. The original mansion was burned down in a great fire at the end of the sixteenth century, and today the courtyard is enclosed by dingy houses four to five stories high, so that much of the Corte del Milione is in deep shadow. Two square passageways run into this quadrangle, one from the direction of the Ponte Rialto, and the other from the direction of the Ponte di Marco Polo over the canal that follows the east side of the courtyard.

The Polo family was originally registered in the parish of San Felice some distance away, and the house in the Corte del Milione was probably bought after the return to Venice. To reach the Ca'-Polo you climb the slimy steps by the Ponte di Marco Polo, leaving your gondola and its bored owner rocking gently in the dirty green water. Over the Marco Polo bridge, which is a recent brick construction, and through the dank Sottoportico, you find yourself in the plain courtyard. There in the opposite corner stands the archway which you have come to see. Its Italo-Byzantine style of the thirteenth century seems incongruous amongst the tall brick façades with their small oblong windows. In the doorway's ornamentation is a crude representation of the Great Roc carrying away a sheep in its talons. Perhaps Marco Polo himself ordered that picture to be inscribed. The barman of the little cafe on the corner of the Sottoportico proudly tells you that he lives in the self-same house as the Il Milione, and so little is left to the memory of Polo that one does not have the heart to refute him.

To Venice

As we returned to our gondola, a small plaque fixed to the wall
of the canal caught our eye. It read*

Qui Furono le Case
di
MARCO POLO
Che viaggio le piu lontane regioni dell' Asia
e le descrisse.

———

per decreto del commune
MDCCCLXXXI

The inscription was put up there at the instigation of the Venice
International Geographical Congress, and it is very nearly all the
recognition that Marco Polo receives from his own city.

There are a few other traces of the great traveller. During the
years that followed his captivity in Genoa and until his death on
January 8th 1324, his name is supposedly mentioned three times
in the Great Book of Maggior Consiglio. On April 13th 1302
there is an entry which states that one Marco Polo was exempted
from the penalty incurred for failing to have a water conduit
examined as provided by law, 'since he was ignorant of the ordi-
nance on the subject'. If this is, indeed, a reference to Il Milione,
it is a warmly human observation that after passing most of his
life in Cathay, Marco overlooked the details of local sanitary bye-
laws. Then on April 10th 1305 Marco stood surety for one
Bonocio of Mestre, a convicted wine-smuggler who was fined 152
lira in four instalments. In the last reference to Polo in the city
records a hint of Marco's journey is introduced when it is written
that he sued one Paulo Girordo, a commission agent, for the price
of half a pound of musk which he had sold on Marco's behalf.
Furthermore the agent had also failed to return one-sixth of the
unsold portion of the merchandise. The case was later decided in
favour of Polo, and Marco was awarded full costs as well, a fair
verdict for the man who in his book informed Europe of the true
origin of musk.

Despite all the rumours of his great wealth, the dry evidence of

*Here was the house of Marco Polo who travelled through the
farthest countries of Asia and described them––by decree of the
commune 1881.

the adventurer's Will points only to comfortable prosperity, which may be explained by a suggestion that the Polos lost heavily in overseas investments at Trebizond. Marco's Will was drawn up by the notary Guistiani, and in it the dying man directed that Pietro his Tartar slave should be set free, and that his worldly goods be divided equally among his daughters after various amounts had been set aside for the Church and his widow's allowance. Marco's children in due course married into the foremost families of Venice, Bragadin, Querini, Dolfin and Gradenigo, but we hear no more of Marco Polo himself. His body was buried in the portico of the old church of San Lorenzo, which was later destroyed, so that no trace is now left even of his burial place. But the best monument to his death is indestructible; the tale attributed to his last days by Jacopo of Acqui. For when the nobles of Venice came to say goodbye to Marco as he lay on his deathbed, they asked him to retract at least some of the amazing stories he had told.

'I have not told the half of it,' was the great traveller's reply.

3

THE BALKANS AND ISTANBUL

WHEN THE MARCO POLO ROUTE PROJECT left Venice, we were already ten days behind schedule. There had been no research to do in the city itself, for Venice and the city's Public Records, being easily accessible, have been closely studied by the great authorities on Polo. By contrast, our trip was concerned with those far-flung segments of the route that had been too distant for easy inspection by the scholars. So in Venice we contented ourselves with filming what we could of Polo's past, and then turned our motorcycles away from Italy and set off on the long loop through Trieste, Yugoslavia and Bulgaria to Turkey. Our investigation of the Polo route would really begin on the high Anatolian plateau of Turkey. Marco, when he had set out for China, had gone first of all to Jerusalem to obtain Holy Oil from the monks at the Sepulchre. A sample of Holy Oil had been specially requested by the Great Khan, for such mystic relics were held in high esteem by medieval peoples. It was an age when the Roman Emperor of Constantinople could raise foreign exchange by selling off such assorted articles as the Crown of Thorns, Jesus' baby linen, and the lance, spear and sponge of the Crucifixion, together with the reed of Moses and a fragment of John the Baptist's skull. Having collected a flask of Holy Oil, the Polos took ship again and sailed to the port of Layas on the southern coast of Turkey. At Layas they said farewell to the maritime influence of their native city and resolutely turned their faces eastward along the land trail that meandered from city to city wherever trade was profitable and the caravans could pass.

With no Polian research to carry out along the Balkan leg of our journey, the run through Yugoslavia was plain, straightforward holiday-making. We were glad to be putting Europe behind us, and felt more confident about our motorcycles. The worries and cares of preparing our trip were over, and as Peter Fleming, one of our mentors, had said so accurately, 'The success of a trip of this nature depends upon the spirit in which it is tackled'. Somehow Mike had got hold of the expedition's maps again, and as a result, instead of proceeding direct to Ljubljana, we took a side-road and found ourselves at Ajeka. This time Stan and I did not complain about Mike's powers of navigation, for we had missed the dull autoput from Ljubljana to Zagreb, and instead, as dusk was gathering, came down to Ajeka across the lovely hills that overlook the Adriatic. That night we spent in a small village off the main road, and started off again next morning while the dew was still on the grass. It was haymaking time all over Yugoslavia, as we roared down the long straight roads towards Belgrade with harvest midges and other winged insects smashing themselves into smears on our goggles. On each side the great plain stretched flat beneath a blazing sun, and everywhere lines of peasants moved in rows across the fields. Tall, powerful men, bare and brown to the waist, marched in steady united rhythm as they wielded their great scythes. Lines of rakers followed some distance behind, and with each group stood the homely shape of the ungainly hay waggon with its team of horses. In the fading of the evening the tall uncut hay rustled in ripples across the wide fields, and on the short stiff stalks where the mowers had passed oxen and horses grazed amongst swirling clouds of gnats.

In Belgrade we became the centre of huge and intensely interested crowds. Whenever we stopped the motorcycles, two or three hundred people would gather around, some to bombard us with questions or offer glasses of slivovitz, while others peered excitedly at the motorbikes. Yugoslavia is very much the land of the motorcycle, and we were constantly meeting enthusiastic motorcyclists who were over-joyed at being able to examine one of the celebrated English machines. On these occasions Mike enjoyed himself hugely, for he would chatter away in rapid pseudo-Cockney accompanying himself with wild gesticulations and finish up triumphantly with his pockets full of cigarettes and his eyes sparkling from glass after glass of slivovitz which his fascinated audience thrust upon him.

On our first evening in Belgrade we dined extravagantly at the flashy Western-style restaurant on the heights overlooking the city. Whilst we ate, the suitcase containing our cine film material was stolen from our machines in the guarded car park. This was a disaster, and although the area soon swarmed with sinister black, diesel-engined, Mercedes Benz patrol cars, the thief could not be traced. We spent a miserable night, and next morning cabled our Home Agent for spare film to be flown to Istanbul to await collection. But we could do nothing to recover the hard work we had already put in on filming the trip so far; most of the exposed material had been stolen and our efforts were wasted.

Angry at ourselves for leaving the machines unattended, we rode southward out of Belgrade. Our bad luck was not yet complete. Mike, who had been learning to drive, crashed his machine whilst coming down a steeply winding mountain road; this time it was Stan who was in the sidecar. We had not gone much more than twenty-five kilometres from Belgrade when the accident happened, so Stan drove back to the city on the remaining motorcycle to fetch help. Meanwhile Mike and I awaited his return confidently, for we knew that Stan was at his best when faced with the problem of organizing other people into doing something that he wanted. We had noticed this phenomenon time and again when the expedition had been held up for want of some small detail or other. A favourite pastime was to ask Stan to obtain bread in some small wretched-looking village where no baker's shop could be seen and where we did not even speak the local dialect. Like a huge bear, Stan would roll into the darkened doorway of a peasant's hut, and gruff grunts were heard from inside. Then Stan's tousled head would re-appear as he emerged blinking from the scene of operations, clutching a large loaf to his chest and often bearing other local delicacies as well. He seemed to take the whole exercise so nonchalantly that we never inquired how he managed the whole thing without ever parting with any money.

As ever, Stan excelled himself. After a few hours he returned from Belgrade on a very ancient pick-up truck in the company of its very, very drunken crew and a beautiful ballerina! The latter had been given a lift en route and was highly decorative, but useless, whilst the truck's crew were not even decorative. They had been enticed away from their homes by Stan's blandishments and on the way had stopped at every opportunity for powerful fortifiers. The scene, as we attempted to load the battered motorcycle and sidecar onto the lorry in the late twilight, was pure comic opera. The befuddled Serbs placed two planks against the truck's tailboard to act as ramps. Then, when our precious machine was halfway up, the planks slipped away and the sidecar fell down with a shattering crash. On the second attempt we made sure that the planks were firmly positioned, but this time, when the motorcycle combination was halfway up, the lorry quietly slid away from under the planks and went careering off down the hill. Above the noise of our machine nosediving onto the road in a repeat performance, we could hear the two Serbs screaming insults at each other for forgetting to set the lorry's handbrake. This exchange of recriminations was only brought to a halt by a dull thud farther down the road as their precious lorry came to rest against a brick wall.

Finally we recovered the lorry, loaded our machines on board and set out in the darkness along the winding mountain road back to Belgrade. The journey was a nightmare, for not only was the roadworthiness of the lorry highly suspect, but its headlights had been effectively obliterated earlier in the evening. This did not deter our Serbian friends in any way at all, even though the driver was in such a state of intoxication that he kept on getting his arms entwined in the spokes of the steering wheel, while the vehicle tore round the hairpin bends at full speed. The members of the expedition clung for dear life to the crazy super-structure of the truck, as we fought with brute strength to hold down the motorcycle which threatened to slide overboard at any moment and shoot off into space when the lorry's tail hung tantalizingly out over the mountain shoulder of the road. Naturally, we stopped for more slivovitz, and yet somehow we were all still in one piece when we reached a garage on the outskirts of Belgrade.

Once more the Marco Polo Route Project was back in Belgrade, heartily sick of the city and condemned to a further frustrating halt while we waited for the motorcycle and its sidecar to be repaired. The garage where we left the machines was a depot for the hard-worked lorries and buses that belonged to the State Transport Services. However it was not so much the repair of public vehicles which delayed the only available mechanic from attending to our needs; the real trouble was that he spent the whole of every morning washing down and polishing an enormous bulbous limousine which belonged to a Party Chief. The little mustachioed mechanic's name was Popovitch, and with him was a sour-looking individual who never opened his mouth in our presence. This character's name was never mentioned, but we were told he was a key Communist, Russian trained and a strong Party man. Whilst the key Communist looked on, Popovitch eventually started repairing the bent sidecar. Now the Serbo-Croatian idea of repairing anything seems to be to belabour it very hard with a sledge hammer. This method is crude, but in certain situations most effective. Above all, it is quick, so once he had actually started on the job, Popovitch soon fixed things up, after which he and I decided to go for a victory spin down the main street. While I mounted on one machine, Popovitch rode the other and the Ubiquitous Communist climbed up behind him, presumably to check up on any capitalist deviations. During the race I managed to edge into the lead and when a tram forced me to brake suddenly, Popovitch, naturally enough, crashed heavily into the rear of my machine. Turning round with a sinking heart, it was immediately clear that a further dose of the Serbian sledge-hammer technique was required. The only consolation was that our tight-lipped Communist fellow-traveller had at last broken silence and was hopping furiously around as he shrieked a stream of curses at the capitalist machine which had struck him a sharp blow on the knee-cap.

In an attempt to cheer ourselves up whilst the machines went back for repairs, the three of us took a bus ride a few kilometres out to a fair at Avala. The fairground was at the top of a small hill where stands a monument to the Unknown Resistance Fighter, or 'The Ignorant Partisan', as we were charmingly misinformed. From the hill you could look out over well-cultivated fields to the junction of the Danube and the Save where they meet at the site of an old Roman camp to flow on as one river to the Black Sea. The fête itself was a disappointment. The stalls displayed the same cheap rubbish which is found in fair grounds all over the world, and the menfolk were drab in grey hats and nylon shirts through which their vests were all too visible. The festivities only livened up when the band began to play and the women in national dress of white blouses, full skirts, scarves and embroidered aprons, linked arms to dance in a great swaying circle. More and more people joined in and soon the whole crowd was broken into circles of dancers moving in a rhythmic repetitive shuffle-step.

Next morning, impatient to be on our way, we called in early at the garage, but to our dismay Popovitch and one of the motor-cycles were missing. Furious, we tracked down the Popovitch home in a dusty suburb. There we found his wife in tears, barely able to speak through her sobs. With one expressive gesture, her hand came forward and turned an imaginary, but very conclusive, key. There was no doubt that poor Popovitch had been locked up under a serious charge. So we went to the enormous grey barracks of Police Headquarters, 29th November Street. Inside, we were conducted along gloomy passages and past doors with the paint flaking from them, until we were finally ushered into the office of the Chief of Section III, Investigations. Behind an alarmingly empty desk under the usual picture of Marshal Tito sat a very tough-looking official. The translator stated our case and a quick telephone call was made. Some minutes later Popovitch was escorted in. The poor fellow looked utterly worn out and terrified. He had been using our motorcycle to get home at the end of his day's work when he had been arrested on suspicion of having stolen the machine. He beseeched us to verify his story, and he was so completely pathetic that we sprang to his defence with some very sharp comments about the whole situation. In the end we took Popovitch back to his home, and he was literally crying with gratitude when he moistly kissed us goodbye, and we went our way, sombrely reflecting on police procedures.

The last few miles into Bulgaria were covered over appalling roads with huge pot-holes which succeeded in pounding to pieces the so-called 'heavy duty' motorcycle panniers, and opening cracks along the body of the passenger sidecar so that it looked like an over-ripe banana splitting at the seams. Indeed it was in such a sorry state that it had become very dangerous, and the third man was forced to ride pillion passenger on the motorcycle pulling the stores sidecar. By doing this, we found that the spare man could in fact rest from the exhausting work of handling the cumbersome machines by lashing his shoulders with rope to the top of the stores sidecar and tying his feet to the motorcycle. In this strange elongated position we were tired enough to snatch a few hours sleep oblivious to the dust, the jolting and the roar of the engine.

Rather to our surprise, once inside Bulgaria the roads improved, and we were soon in Sofia, where we called at the offices of the student newspaper. From there we were taken to see the new University buildings, the new Spor Palas and the student dormitories. It was all very clean and dedicated, but somehow we felt that we preferred the fusty rooms of our Oxford colleges, from where we could spend our vacations following Marco Polo's route and not labouring in the State Work Brigades. Nevertheless, we were much impressed by the kindliness of our hosts and their eagerness to show their country off to the best advantage, feeding us on pilau in the student cafeteria and talking earnestly about their future. We also found time to visit the exquisite Byzantine Church of St. Sophia, where research workers were still opening up early Christian vaults. Legend has it that the Emperor Constantine fell in love with his sister Sophia. Wishing to possess her, he pursued her through the town. She fled to the place where the present church of St. Sophia now stands, and there in a blue mist she disappeared into a chasm in the earth. And even now she is sometimes to be seen at the dead of night as a ghostly blue apparition in front of the place which gave her refuge from her incestuous and imperious lover.

Our last stop in Sofia was the shopping centre, which turned out to be a very large, ugly, square, supermarket. The shelves were well stocked, but such essentials as sugar seemed very expensive. Stan however, startled even the hardened shop assistants, long accustomed as they are to simple local standards of food, when he demanded a kilo of mashed offal intended as dog food, and then began munching it on the spot. Mike and I preferred the more usual Bulgarian café diet of eggs pickled in brown wine followed by numerous hay-filled cigarettes.

Our passage through Bulgaria was very brief, and it was not long before we were driving past the profusion of Army pickets which guard the roads leading up to the border with Turkey. The first sight of the frontier is very impressive. The control point is dominated by a tall concrete watch-tower rather like a water tank. Above the tower floats the star and crescent of Turkey, and beneath the flag stands the pugnacious figure of a Turkish soldier. From head to foot he is dressed in American battle dress, and he carries his American-made automatic rifle with calm assurance. We had seen a great many soldiers in Bulgaria, but the efficient toughness of the Turkish sentry as he stared down at us through his binoculars impressed us enormously, and in a way this impression lasted with us for as long as we were in the country.

Turkey-in-Europe from the frontier to Edirne and on to Istanbul is dull and dusty. The rolling country is dry and meagre, and although from time to time you pass modern petrol stations, they are all but deserted. There are no cars on the gravel roads, only convoys of army lorries filled with more of the hard-looking soldiery in their stained, crumpled denims. There are hardly any settlements by the roadside, only the occasional flock of scraggy sheep, herded by an old man or a small boy, always carrying a cudgel and wearing an enormous greasy flat cap very like a strange overgrown cousin to the caps which are so popular in the industrial towns of Northern England. Every fifteen miles or so, the road runs past a stark army encampment with soldiers drilling endlessly in front of the tents, and over to one side wait huge blocks of neatly parked American lorries drawn up in squares of a hundred or more vehicles each. The minarets of Edirne hardly break the monotony; only the forlorn signpost standing in the central cross roads of the town captures the spirit of the district. On its three pointing arms are written 'Istanbul'; 'Greece'; and 'Bulgaria'.

It was afternoon when we eventually caught sight of the Sea of Marmora, and we really felt our journey had begun as we topped the final hill and below us saw Istanbul, the city that has had such influence on the lives of so many empires and so many people. By some it has been called the capital of the world, and in Marco Polo's age it was the richest of prizes when Venice strove against Genoa to gain control of the great commercial focus where Asia meets Europe.

From these hills above the city in 1204 the wily Doge Dandolo

38

had persuaded an abortive Crusade to turn against Constantinople and not against the Infidel. French and Venetian troops took
the city by storm, and after the subsequent looting many of the
spoils were carried back to grace the squares of Venice where they
can still be seen. The Doge himself could not leave Venice to rule
the portion of Constantinople which was part of the loot, so in his
place a regent was appointed to govern the Venetian colony, which
was granted its own laws and trading privileges. The Doge himself took the title of Prince of Rumania, and half a century later
the city played a crucial part in the very story of Marco Polo's
trip, for in his book he writes that : —

> In the year of Our Lord 1260, when Baldwin was Emperor of
> Constantinople and Messer Ponte governed the city in the name
> of the Doge of Venice, Messer Nicolo Polo, the father of Marco,
> and Messer Maffeo, who was Nicolo's brother, were in that city
> having come there from Venice with their merchandise. They
> were men of good family, remarkable for their wisdom and
> foresight. After discussing various matters, they made up their
> minds that they would go across the Black Sea in the hope of
> a profitable venture. So they bought many jewels of great
> beauty and price, and set out from Constantinople by ship and
> went to Sudak.

A wealth of important meaning lies beneath this terse narrative
of Marco's. His father and uncle 'remarkable for their wisdom
and foresight' had no illusions about the precarious nature of
Venetian influence at Constantinople after the death of the force-
ful Doge Dandolo. Baldwin II, Count of Flanders and cousin to
Louis IX of France, had but one year left to reign before his
departure from the scene as the last Latin Emperor of Constantinople. The Venetian Regent Ponte had little effective power to
protect Venice's interests, and the Genoese colony was arrogantly
reflecting the growing might of their own State. As a result the
business community was distinctly jittery, and there is little doubt
that these were the sort of problems which Nicolo and Maffeo
worried about as they 'discussed various matters'. It was in the
finest tradition of mercantile Venetians that they decided to sell
the Polo holdings in Constantinople, and then converted their
capital into precious gems which were at a glut in the lavish city
markets, at that time depressed by the mutterings of the impend-

The Balkans and Istanbul

ing political storm. The upshot was that the Polos abandoned Constantinople and sailed north to Sudak on the Black Sea, from whence they set out on their first tentative trip which led them even farther afield to the Court of the Great Khan. Behind them, Venetian influence in Constantinople finally crumbled in front of the Byzantine Genoese onslaught, and by the time that Maffeo and Nicolo returned from their wanderings Venetian aspirations in the area had fallen back to their trading factories at Negropont in Greece. Thus it was that the vicissitudes of Constantinople were among the root causes of Marco Polo's fantastic wanderings.

In its essential characteristics the city can hardly have changed since Polo's own time, for no tides of political fortune can take away the basic intermingling of peoples that gives Istanbul so much of its atmosphere. It was a stirring impression as the road carried us into the city under a huge arch in the towering rampart walls of Topkapu that still conjure up visions of besieging armies. Even so, these fortifications themselves are only lifeless relics when contrasted with the bustle of scores of nationalities across Galata Bridge near the Golden Horn. The babble of tongues and the kaleidoscope of racial dress and features would be instantly recognizable to Marco Polo himself. For us, there was no city that we had visited which was so striking in its immediate appeal to the traveller.

Now it was the established practice of our little group to carry all our money reserves in the form of American dollar bills, as all three of us during earlier journeying had grown to appreciate the comparative ease with which one can change dollar bills into local currency in areas where Traveller's Cheques or the pound sterling are hardly known. In Sofia we had been forced to carry out our money-changing operations in a most furtive fashion with a Black Marketeer, who insisted on completing the transaction in the middle of a field some miles from the city. But in Istanbul the problem was much simpler. We drove straight to the Black Market area at the back of Taksim Square, and parking the motorcycles, merely sat down on the kerb beside them and waited for the never-failing attentions of that international brand of spiv who battens upon foreign visitors. Sure enough, a voice behind us asked the classic opening, 'Can I help you?' and we turned to see an intelligent-looking young Turk of about our own age, dressed in

40

cheap, but very clean and well pressed, clothes, who was regarding us without the usual furtive air of the Black Market operator. We introduced ourselves and explained that we wanted to change some of our money into Turkish lira. Arghun, for that was the young man's name, explained that under the new military Government of Turkey, it was no longer worthwhile to change money on the Black Market, as the Banks would pay the same exchange rate. 'But,' said Arghun, 'perhaps we would like to go back to his home with him, if we had nowhere else to stay in Istanbul.' The invitation was startlingly direct and it took some time for us to overcome our suspicions, but before long we realized that in Arghun we had found a friend and helper who, with his family, made the popular ideas of Eastern hospitality seem like pale imitations of the truth. Above all, it was through Arghun's help that we saw Istanbul as the city really is, behind the façade which it usually presents to the tourist.

First we went back to Arghun's home at Number Four, Madirge Sokak, Feridige, Istanbul. We turned the motorcycles away from the boulevards of central Istanbul, and vanished into the maze of tiny alleys that lace the huge sprawling quarter of the city that covers the hill sloping down to the Golden Horn. This is the home of the hundreds of thousands of Turks who are at the lower end of the social scale; the cigarette-sellers, shoe-cleaners, taxi-drivers, bazaar-stall-holders and others like them. Arghun's family were watersellers who owned a tiny basement shop up near Taksim Square. The entire family lived in four small rooms of a little tenement house which huddled into the side of a cobbled alley so steep that we did not dare take the motorcycles down it, but had to leave them at the top. Naturally we were rather worried about leaving our heavily loaded machines unguarded, but Arghun assured us that they would be perfectly safe. He was absolutely right, for the moment it was known throughout the quarter that we had come as guests, our motorcycles were as safely watched as if we had left them locked up at the Central Police Station. By day, the swarms of small children that climbed all over them discouraged interference, and throughout the nights that followed, an aged grandmother was always noticeable somewhere in a darkened doorway, a shadowy figure sitting quietly within sight of our precious machines, ready to raise the hue and cry.

Next we were introduced to Arghun's family, headed of course by Poppa, an impressive figure with the growl of a bear and a heart of gold. He ruled the family as its lord and master. His scowl would send the children scurrying and even stir Momma into action. Great fat Momma was wonderful, she had raised six children of her own and now she found room to adopt three wandering strangers. She asked Poppa's permission to have one of the two groundfloor rooms vacated, and this was turned into our home for the next two weeks. Arghun's four sisters started in on the task of looking after us, a task which they executed in a hundred different ways from washing our hair to actually popping food into our mouths as we ate. The girls had the most wonderful names, like Isel which means 'moon and much rain' and Icon or 'blood and moon'. Our favourite by far was the youngest sister called Mokartez which means 'mystery', but we called her Mickey Mouse, as she won a place in all our hearts with her cheerfulness and the dedication with which she looked after us. I shall never forget seeing her climbing up the alley, a slender little figure with long hair falling about her shoulders, nearly dwarfed by a pair of our long motorcycle boots which she was carrying to the shoe-cleaning man.

We were so tired and dirty when we arrived at Arghun's house, that the family insisted we should have a bath. This meant going along to the Public Baths, and naturally, as we were in Turkey, these were true Turkish baths. Such places have their imitations in other lands, but to have a real Turkish bath you must go to the country itself, and pay a little over a penny at the turnstile in the entrance to one of the many Public baths. Inside, one is ordered about by an attendant Turk wearing only a red and green towel around his waist and a pair of wooden sandals on his feet. A few moments later you emerge from a little cubicle in the same dress, and are then escorted through two different sets of doors which act as a sort of valve, letting you into the steam-filled atmosphere of the bathing rooms. Here we wandered about in a twilight scene. Overhead the roof curved up like an inverted bowl to a glass panel which let in the half-light. The walls and floors were of worn black marble, and everywhere hot water flowed from fountains and basins in the wall, from deep pools in the floor and over slabs of marble carved into seats. For well over an hour we revelled in the pleasures of bathing, then we lay down on a steaming marble slab and were pummelled and punched by masseurs. Finally we dressed and left the baths more refreshed and relaxed than we had believed possible after our exhaustion earlier in the day.

Soon it was supper time, so Arghun took us back home for the first of many happy and exotic meals. The family sat around the single table under Poppa's watchful eye. The three guests flanked him, and everyone else squeezed in wherever possible, sitting on old chairs or one of the beds which was drawn up as a bench. Meals at Arghun's home followed a distinct pattern. Breakfast was Turkish cheese, bread, tomatoes, sausages cut up into small pieces and salami. Lunch and dinner were made up of an infinite variety of Turkish dishes, beans, rice, stripped vegetables, salted cucumber, peppers and fruit; especially fruit, quantities and quantities of peaches, apricots, grapes, plums and nuts. At any time during the meal, one could expect a neighbour to select a particularly delectable morsel from your own or his plate and pop it into your mouth with his fingers. Poppa soon got to know us well enough to take a mouth-burning pepper on the sly and push it into your open mouth when you were off guard. Then as you struggled to swallow it, he would roar with laughter till the tears rolled down his face, matching the tears that were streaming down from his victim's eyes. Buying food and preparing it was left entirely to the older daughters, as was the washing up, for that was the sacred time for Çay. Turkish tea, or Çay, is delicious, and Poppa had an iron rule that in his house it should be prepared perfectly. The tea leaves, not from India, but from Persia, were boiled in the copper kettle for just the right length of time, and the hot golden liquid poured into tiny delicate glasses over two or three lumps of sugar. The drink that resulted was excellent and we menfolk sat around talking for hours, sipping glass after glass of Poppa's admirable Çay and filling the air with the smoke of the local cheap Turkish cigarettes.

As Arghun was temporarily out of work, the family's entire income came from the little water shop near Taksim Square. The piped water in Istanbul is of poor quality, but perfectly drinkable. Many Turks, however, prefer to drink the sweeter water that comes from the local wells, which are owned by private companies. These in turn market their water in smaller bottles and sell them to customers for a few pence. Indeed many Turks in Istanbul can taste water in the same way as we might taste wine, only the Turk would be concerned not with the vintage, but with the name and character of the well from which the water was drawn.

Every morning Poppa would dress up in a white-and-blue striped shirt and crisp flannels which he hitched up until his socks could be seen in all their elegance between the turnups and his highly polished shoes of black and white Italian leather. He would tighten his belt a notch in anticipation of a hard day's work, and make sure he had a packet of his favourite Yeni Harman cigarettes in the breast pocket of his shirt. A final scowl at the children, so that they would not forget to carry out their duties for the day, and Poppa would stamp out of the door past the huge pile of wooden slippers which we all had to wear indoors, leaving our outdoor shoes on the mat. Poppa leisurely climbs the cobbled path to Taksim Square where the café tables have already been put out opposite his shop. Here Poppa greets his cronies and stops for a glass of Çay; one glass follows after another and for Poppa this is his working day. Very occasionally he stumps across the road to peer in at the doorway to his shop. Inside one of his daughters, usually Isel, busies herself with sweeping an already spotless floor. In fact, Isel handles any customers who call in, and all day long Poppa sits at the other side of the street, a glass of Çay in front of him, or he saunters up and down, passing the time of day with the other shopowners who seem to enjoy the same relaxed approach to business.

Arghun's family did most of its shopping in the huge covered bazaar on the far side of Galata Bridge. To get there, one either boarded an ancient tram which clangs its way along the narrow paved streets, or one could use Istanbul's own Underground Transport system. This unusual arrangement consisted of two trains running in two steep shafts that link the top and bottom of the hill that overlooks the Golden Horn. The two trains operate rather like a pair of spiders. As one train hauls itself up to the top of the hill by winding in on a long cable, its opposite number releases the handbrake and suddenly drops down the slope trailing its cable behind it. The other cheap method of getting about the city is to take a Dolmus taxi. This is a sort of hitch-hiking in city traffic. Arghun, who was naturally an expert at the game, would stroll

44

along the middle of the road shouting out his destination to the stream of huge old-fashioned American cars, which serve as the taxis in Istanbul. If one of the taxi drivers happened to be going the same way, he would clap on the brakes and, as his battered taxi squealed to a halt, we would clamber quickly in on top of his previous load of passengers. The taxi would then lurch on its way, diving into the smallest of gaps and taking no notice at all of the hundreds of military policemen in their red and white striped helmets, who attempted to direct traffic at every possible inter-section. Every now and again our driver would swerve over to the pavement in order to cry out his destination to a likely looking passenger or to drop off one of his compressed fares. Whenever anyone got out, the driver would make a rough estimate of the person's share of the journey to that particular point, and this seldom came to more than a shilling or so.

The Great Bazaar was a world in itself. It seemed that there was nothing which could not be bought or sold within the vast, sprawling network of alleys, filled with their jostling crowds. Various of Arghun's cousins owned stalls in the bazaar, and we could sit in them for hours watching the colourful flood of people, talking in a dozen different languages and drawn from every mixture of race and religion. Especially noticeable were the many bazaar porters dressed in sackcloth and pushing in front of them the two-wheeled carts that are used to move merchandise from stall to stall. Everywhere there were waterboys with huge brass flasks on their backs, and in one hand a tin cup which they rattled against the flask in the hopes of attracting custom, or wandering shoe-cleaners with their trays of brass-tipped bottles, each tray a complete shop in miniature with every shade of polish, wax and oil represented, so that even our scuffed and battered motorcycle boots were given a deep glowing shine after a few minutes hard work with brush and polishing cloth. It was in the Bazaar that we had some huge thick leather camel-bags made up in a leather worker's shop to replace our useless modern fibreglass panniers. The camel-bags were heavy and smelled deliciously of semi-cured leather, and in the end they lasted the whole length of our trip through flood and desert. It seemed that there are some things for which no substitute has been found since the caravan days of Polo.

Then there was the gipsy quarter of Istanbul, which the police

45

patrols dared not enter after dark. But Arghun took us there to see the enchanting dances performed by the children, when you can get them away from their mistrustful grown-ups. One morning as we passed by the gipsy village on our way to Taksim Square, we were lucky enough to come across a gipsy wedding in full swing. It was only an hour or so after dawn, but already the long tables had been set up in the alley and loaded with fruit and coloured fizzy drinks of various kinds in addition to the usual bottles of liquor. Soon the tables were filled with gipsies in all their finery, rings in their ears, flowers in their hair, and, for once, a smile for everyone. Two fiddlers and a man with a wooden instrument, rather like a large shepherd's pipe, provided the music and everywhere scampered little gipsy children with grimy faces and dark brown hair streaked with gold. Now and again someone would jump to their feet and dance towards the bridal pair, snatching up a wreath from the table or from the head of another guest, and with it crown the bride or her groom.

On the second to last day in Istanbul, I managed to obtain an audience with the Governor of Istanbul Province. He is in fact one of the most important men in the country and treated with a very great deal of awe and respect, for he is not only the Governor of the city, but also the Commander of the Turkish Armies which control the city and its approaches. Our only card of entry to see this very busy man was a front page article in the local prestige newspaper about the Marco Polo Route Project. Armed with this, I insisted that Arghun should go with me, for he had done so much for us that in return I felt we could do this little for him. Together we entered the gigantic governor's Palace and were escorted through halls, chambers and ante-rooms, filled with bustling secretaries or generals and city elders sitting awaiting audience with the great man himself. In due course and after much waving of our precious newspaper, we were ushered into the Governor's drawing room. There the Governor himself greeted us very hospitably and we spent an amusing half-hour talking and drinking coffee. Finally we rose to leave, and started back between the long lines of waiting dignitaries over whom we had taken precedence. Then and only then I confided to Arghun that from start to finish of our visit to the Palace, he had forgotten to tuck his shirt-tails inside his trousers.

The Balkans and Istanbul

Finally the day came when we had to leave Momma and Poppa and the family to set out along Marco Polo's trail with our motorcycles. We crossed the Bosphorus on one of the ferries that shuttle back and forth across the strip of water that divides Europe and Asia, and on the Asian side we said goodbye to Arghun who in traditional fashion had crossed with us so that he might come along the first part of the departing guest's road. As we drove off, there were tears in Arghun's eyes, and there was no doubt in our minds that all of us would one day go back to see again that wonderful Turkish family.

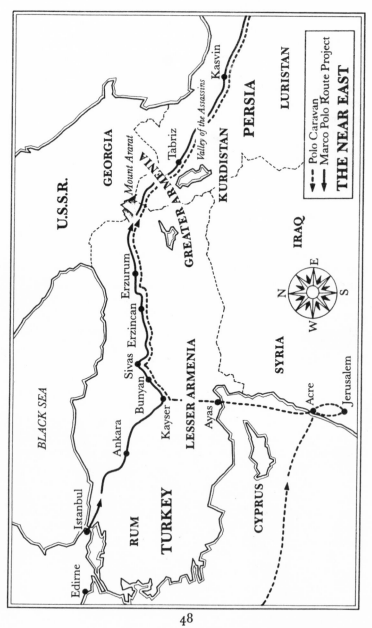

THE NEAR EAST

- - - - Polo Caravan
——— Marco Polo Route Project

U.S.S.R.

GEORGIA

BLACK SEA

Edirne

Istanbul

RUM

TURKEY

Ankara

Sivas Erzincan Erzurum

Bunyan

Kayser

LESSER ARMENIA

Ayas

CYPRUS

Mount Ararat

GREATER ARMENIA

Tabriz

Valley of the Assassins

Kasvin

KURDISTAN

PERSIA

LURISTAN

IRAQ

SYRIA

Acre

Jerusalem

N
W E
S

4

MARCO POLO'S LESSER
ARMENIA

THE GREEKS GAVE THE NAME ANATOLIA to the plateau
country of Turkey-in-Asia. To the Hellenes, the barren upland
that rises behind the populous coastal plain where the Greek city
colonies thrived, was a separate country, Anatolia or the land 'to
the East'. Even today there is a pronounced change in atmosphere
as the road drives inland and climbs into the harsh tableland. The
settlements along the way gradually dwindle in size and are yet
further apart, huddling on the safety of easily defensible mounds,
a sure sign of recently unsettled conditions. The New Turkey has
only just begun to push the savage frontier back, as the European
way of life flows along the main roads and radiates from the larger
towns. Ankara itself stands as an example of this movement. In
Polo's day the site of the Turkish capital was nothing more than
a village which can be traced back to Hittite times. But it was here
that Ataturk, Father of Turkey, based his centre of campaign
communications during the fight against the powers associated
with the decadence of Istanbul. And when Ataturk had won his
victory, the ancient Hittite village was proclaimed the country's
capital, an artificial creation for political reasons, so that even now
it is said that 'only fools and Deputies leave Constantine's capital
for Ataturk's'.

Not least among the reasons for Ankara's unpopularity is the
raw continental climate of Anatolia, which Marco Polo described
as being 'far from healthy; it is in fact, extremely enervating'. In

summer the plateau is scorching hot, and in winter many areas are made impassable by deep snow. Typical of this inhospitable climate are the violent summer thunderstorms, bringing moisture which is only a partial blessing to the desiccated land, for the heavy rain is soon swallowed up by the cracked earth, but not before the deluge has sluiced away the shallow topsoil and washed out the gravel roads. The fringes of the tableland are particularly exposed to these storms, many of which are drawn in from the sea and condense as they rise up the flanks of the plateau. We found that driving through one of these thunderstorms was very much like travelling underwater. The motorcycles kept going bravely, but both we and our equipment were soon soaked through. In the heart of each downpour visibility was reduced to nil, and on one occasion Stan ran full tilt into the tail of a column of soldiers marching stoically along like a huge tarpaulin centipede.

Luckily we had a chance to dry out on the run into Ankara itself, for the belt of rainstorms did not extend over the lip of the upland, and the sun scorched down on a dusty road. We were not to know it then, but with one exception it did not rain again during our journey until we ran into the Indian monsoon half a continent away. From Ankara to the Khyber Pass, the common factor which linked us with the conditions of Polo's day, and which dominated the lives of Afghans, Turks, Persian, and alike was the lack of rainfall. On this single criterion we had reached Marco Polo's Asia.

Our stay in Ankara was largely taken up with visits to the British Embassy to collect our mail and a protracted sortie to the airport in order to pick up cine film which had been flown out to us from England. The Customs officials had the rather disturbing idea that the only way of checking that the film was unexposed was to open the specially sealed containers and hold the strips of celluloid up to the light. At this, Mike got extremely agitated about his precious film stock, and Stan only managed to save the situation by claiming personal relationship not only to the Turkish Minister of the Interior, but also the British Foreign Secretary. In the end the whole matter was sorted out very amicably over long and leisurely cups of sticky coffee provided by courtesy of the Turkish Customs and Excise, and the Marco Polo Route

Project had enough cine film stowed away in the motorcycle panniers to last us until Kabul.

There was no doubt that by now we had become thoroughly pro-Turkish, and were enjoying every minute of our time with Turkish people. In fact, one of our happiest evenings was spent in Ankara at the Youth Park with a group of young Turks of much our own age. With them we made the rounds of the Fun Fair amusements in the Park, Stan exciting awed cries of approval as he nearly broke the machine which provides a test of strength. The evening ended with us all sitting on the shores of the central ornamental lake, smoking from the great tasselled Narghile pipes with their enormous wads of tobacco and charcoal, whilst an electric samovar, an engaging mixture of ancient and modern, bubbled away providing glass after glass of Çay.

The next morning we were once again on our way, riding out of the capital and into the desolate countryside of Anatolia. Our road lay south-west to the village of Topcali on the main route to Kayseri. We plunged straight from the modern bustle and blare of Ankara into the poverty of the plateau. The tiny village of Topcali had little to distinguish it from any of the other clusters of flat-roofed mud shacks which dot the barren countryside. The people live on a meagre diet of beans and vegetables helped out with the very occasional stew made from the carcass of a scraggy horned sheep, flocks of which graze on the sparse shrubs of the hillsides. Occasionally one would see tobacco leaves hung out on the porches of the larger houses, so that the leaf dried and withered in the furnace-like heat. But in the poorer areas even this meagre luxury disappeared, and the flocks of sheep became fewer and fewer.

In Topcali we ate our evening meal, sharing our food with the desperately ragged village children who appeared shyly around us. To withstand the terrible summer heat, the houses themselves are built on the principle of ovens in reverse. They have immensely thick roofs and walls of mud with no windows and only a small hole for a doorway, the aim being to keep out the heat. The floors of the huts were scooped downwards, both to provide mud for building and to help the inhabitants huddle closer into the cool of the earth. No wood could be seen in the construction of their houses, for the highlands are almost completely devoid of usable trees, and every scrap of wood is carefully hoarded to make the crude furniture. But even in this harsh environment the people were not only helpful, but possessed a natural dignity which made up for much of their hardship. It was encouraging proof that, if we looked in the right places, we would find conditions which Marco Polo had described seven hundred years earlier, and which might throw more light on the great traveller's description of his thirteenth century world.

In Marco Polo's age the Turkish uplands formed a cul-de-sac for Asia Minor. Into this region were driven successive waves of races and tribes ousted from their holdings in richer lands further east by more powerful invaders. The peninsula of Turkey was a no-man's-land of strange groups living in close proximity to one another and without any overall unity. The latest wave of invaders had been the Tartars of Genghis Khan and they had driven the earlier tribes, especially the Turks, westward against the defences of Christendom, thereby giving rise to the legend of the Terrible Turk. Polo calls the western end of Turkey 'Karaman', but to the Tartars of the Levant the area was still Rumi, the 'Roman' land, though in reality the Byzantine Empire was too weak to have much control over the region, where the only worthwhile Christian forces were outposts of the Knights Templar. The central area of the peninsula around Sivas was divided into provinces held by the weakened Seljuk dynasty which owed allegiance to the Mongols. To some contemporary chroniclers this was the country of 'Turkomania', feared by the medieval Europeans, for it lay on the overland route to the Holy Land and in their attempts to force a passage through this predominantly Muslim region the Crusading armies had been bled of six hundred thousand men who perished in the wild plateau.

Marco Polo's geographical description of Turkey goes even further back to the classic division used by Ptolemy, who divided the larger part of Anatolia into the two Armenias, the Greater and the Lesser. The latter, Polo says, 'has a king who maintains good and just government in his land which is under the suzerainty of the Tartars'. The rulers of Lesser Armenia were descendants of the first Seljuk ruler, a Turkoman of Turkistan in the service of a Tartar prince on the lower reaches of the Syr Daria. From there he had fled to Transoxania to be joined by Turkoman members of his own family which had ruled over a minor kingdom in Khorassan, a north-eastern Persian province. This branch of Turkomans had then moved westward at the end of the eleventh century and taken Armenia from the Greeks, before in due course falling themselves to the Mongols, who over-ran both Armenias but never really occupied Lesser or Western Armenia.

Thus Marco describes the inhabitants of Lesser Armenia in his day as falling into three races of men.

The Turcomans themselves, who worship Mahomet and keep his law, are a primitive people, speaking a barbarous language. They roam over the mountains and the plains, wherever is good pasturage, for they live off their flocks. They have clothing made of skins, and dwellings of felt or of skins. The country breeds fine Turkan horses and good mules of excellent quality which fetch a good price. The other races are the Armenians and the Greeks who live intermingled among the Turcomans in the villages and towns, and make their living by commerce and crafts. They weave the choicest and most beautiful carpets in the world. They also weave silk fabrics of crimson and other colours, of great beauty and richness, and many other kinds of cloth. Their most celebrated cities are Konya, Kaiseriah and Sivas.

This description of the commercial role of the Armenians and Greeks in Turkey is apt even in this modern age, despite the seven centuries of history since the time that Marco wrote, though the Turcomans have largely settled down to stable agriculture from the typically nomadic way of life that was more widespread throughout the peninsula in Polo's time. Furthermore this passage from *The Description of the World* contained some specific points which we wanted to clear up, as they had baffled the great commentators and scholars of Polian research. In particular we wanted to find more about Marco's puzzling references to the 'fine Turkan horses'; the unusually good mules and the descriptions of silk and carpet weaving.

At Topcali we were on the fringes of Polo's Lesser Armenia and also within striking distance of one of the more extraordinary phenomena which characterized the diversity of medieval Anatolia. Hidden away in the heart of this Muslim province had thrived an outstanding Christian hermit sect at the twin settlements of Urgup and Goreme. Today, the small township of

Urgup is a busy local market centre with its white-washed mud houses climbing up the side of the cliff against which the town is built, so that Urgup has a strangely Moroccan air. But Goreme is more impressive to the visitor, for it remains much as it was in the days of its occupation between the ninth and thirteenth centuries. By the fourteenth century the Christians had fled, leaving their fantastic monuments in the dead valley.

To reach Goreme we turned off the main road and cautiously drove our way along a sand track, for the Southern Turkish Desert is not so far away and the path we followed was more like a North African 'wadi'. Along this dried-up watercourse the landscape closed in about us and took on a weird surrealist air. Huge cones of rock, carved by wind and water, rose like a legion of ant-hills in strange contorted shapes. Red, yellow and brown pillars or pyramids of sandstone towered above us as the track twisted and turned its way between them. To our left lay Mount Argens and behind us the ancient volcano of Hassandag, but in the moon-scape of erosion we felt only a sense of eternity and detachment.

Goreme itself lies in the bottom of a large crater hollowed out of the plateau, and looking down from the rim where the path had led us, we could see on the crater's floor cluster upon cluster of more strange rock pillars, and a little farther away the tell-tale green patch of a watercourse. The road looped sharply downwards into the bowl, and at the bottom we left the motorcycles so that we might explore the hermits' oasis where the holy men had contemplated away their lives in such terrible isolation.

Supposedly there are 365 churches hollowed out of the sandstone columns of Goreme, for each rock cone thrusts upward like a rotten tooth riddled with cavities. We crawled from cavern to cavern, up worn steps and into innumerable passageways and grottoes, till at last we were brought out on a little platform at the very pinnacle of one mound, and could look across at the other pillars with their sockets of cave mouths. Here and there are crumbling Greek inscriptions, deeply carved crosses and even worn, fading coloured murals, all depicting religious figures. The dust settles upon them today as it has done since the time when the Christians mysteriously fled from Goreme, leaving their caves and shrines to the lizards and rock doves beneath the hot white glare and reflection of the bleaching sun. Only at one end of the crater is there human life nowadays; a tiny Mohammedan community has moved into the abandoned caves and leads a troglodite existence where each home is marked with a neat little postal number fixed to the rock by the cave mouth.

As we left Goreme, a bearded horseman rode skilfully down the steep track towards us. He was mounted on a small, but well proportioned, brown horse which looked strangely trim and sleek amidst the bleakness of its surroundings. As the horseman drew level with us, we stopped and asked him what kind of horse he rode. 'This is a Turkan Arab horse,' was the proud reply, 'for I am a headman of the village.' Those few words established with startling simplicity that we stood in Polo's footsteps. Marco had remarked upon the 'fine Turkan horses', and here we too had immediately noticed the magnificence of the animal we had just seen. The Turkish Sultans had always been admirers of good horseflesh, and throughout the length and breadth of their land the finest animals of the native Cappadocian breed had been sought after and brought to the Imperial Stud Farms to be crossed with specially imported Arab horses of the finest quality, many of whom had been presented as gifts to the Sultans by other potentates. Close by where we met our proud Goreme headman had been one of the foremost imperial stud farms at Sultaniya, and we began to understand why it was that Polo after twenty-three years journeying could still remember the Turkan horses when he languished in a Genoese jail.

After this incident we became even more alert to Marco's reference of fine mules, which he had said could be found in Lesser Armenia. Along the roads to Kayseri we saw splendid-looking specimens of mules, usually with glossy white coats. Then, in Kayseri itself, we were fortunate enough to meet one of the few veterinary workers in the province and he was able to tell us more about Polo's 'fine mules which fetch a good price'. We learnt that mules have never been used very much in that part of Turkey and that the animals which we had admired were in fact a special breed of donkey called the Cyprus donkey. This type of donkey, easily mistaken for a mule, is highly valued to this day, for it has a great carrying capacity coupled with low feeding costs and, of course, unlike the mule the ability to breed. There is no way of telling whether Polo too had mistaken the Cyprus donkey for a 'fine mule', but there can be no doubt that the Cyprus donkey with its longer legs, better proportions and flat stomach, has for centuries been the most highly prized beast of burden in the area, commanding a price far higher than either the mule proper or the more normal small donkey. Unfortunately the spread of motor transport is bringing a steady decline in the numbers of Cyprus donkeys, for those people who might afford to buy them are turning more and more to small trucks which they purchase through loans or co-operatives. But the poorer peasants still use the ordinary brown donkey which is cheap and satisfies their more limited needs, and we often came across huge herds of these sorrowful little beasts being driven along the road in their hundreds by professional dealers who travel from village to village marketing their animals.

Kayseri was the first large town to which our route had brought us since leaving Ankara. Only a few mosques and mausoleums remain to bear witness to the town's former days of glory when, with Sivas and Konya, Kayseri was a capital of the Seljuk Empire. Formerly called Mazaca and then compulsorily renamed Caesaria of Cappadocia after annexation by Tiberius in A.D. 17, Kayseri, when Marco Polo came there, still retained its trading importance, as shewn by Marco's note of the silks and cloths woven on the spot by the Armenians and the Greeks. However we could find no trace of the old luxury textile industry except for some dusty, but still gorgeous, tunics on display in the town's museum. The costumes were made from brocaded silk, whose colours are still rich and superb today, but the ornamentation of the beaten gold epaulettes and belt buckles places the workmanship later than Polo in the time of the early Ottoman dynasty. The only consolation was that, according to the Keeper of the Museum, the craftsmanship shewed a dexterity and sophistication which hinted at even earlier weaving and embroidery skills peculiar to the locality.

When the Polos had landed at the great trade emporium of Layas on the southern coast of Lesser Armenia, their caravan had included two friars, who had been allocated to the venture by Pope Gregorius X Placentinus in a somewhat inadequate response to the Great Khan's request for 'a hundred men learned in the Christian religion and well versed in the Seven Arts', the medieval combination of Rhetoric, Logic, Grammar, Arithmetic, Astronomy, Music and Geometry. Marco records that the two clerics were Dominican Friars, by name Brother Nicholas of Vicenza and Brother William of Tripoli, who were entrusted with 'several handsome cases of crystal as gifts to the Great Khan', and were granted licence to ordain priests, consecrate bishops, and grant absolution even as the Pope. Brother William was already famous for a treatise that he had written on Mohammedanism and the Saracens, so perhaps Marco was justified in describing them as 'assuredly the wisest in all that province'. But, whatever their other qualification for the task, the two Friars certainly did not possess the necessary courage to make the hazardous trek across all Asia. Here, in the wild country of Armenia they lost heart and returned to the safety of Christendom, leaving their presents in the care of the Polos for onward transmission to Peking.

The reason for this precipitous flight on the part of the Friars was the rumour that the Silk Road had been cut by raiding parties sent north by Bibars Bundokdari, Sultan of the Mamelukes of Egypt. This courageous warrior, an outstanding Moslem leader of his time, had broken out from Egypt, swept through Syria and captured Jerusalem. Bibars, a man of great energy who was rumoured to have played tennis in both Cairo and Damascus in the same week, had already invaded Armenia once before (1266) and the fall of Antioch before his armies had shaken the Christian world. Now he was harrying northward from his Syrian bases, and it speaks greatly for the bravery and confidence of the Polos that they steadfastly continued their journey in the face of this threat.

For the most part, the modern road out of Kayseri follows the same track as the Old Silk Road, and like the Polos' caravan the Marco Polo Route Project set off along it towards Sivas, formerly called Sebaste (Ptolemy's Sebastopolis). On the way we were interested in visiting the village of Bunyan, for in Kayseri's bazaar we had been told that if we sought the making of carpets we should go to Bunyan. We received this information with a certain amount of scepticism, for Colonel Sir Henry Yule, probably the greatest authority on Marco Polo's journey, had stated that carpets no longer appeared to be produced in the area. Nevertheless, in search of Marco's 'choicest and most beautiful carpets in the world', we turned off the main road some 40 kilometres out of Kayseri, and carried on a farther 12 kilometres down a rough gravel track across rolling countryside to where Bunyan's mud houses stood on the side of a hill. We drove into the village not knowing the Turkish word for carpet, as we had already lost our Turkish dictionary. There was absolutely no sign whatever of any carpet-making in progress, so we attempted to mime our query. Making what we thought were weaving gestures to a group of men who had gathered round our machines, we were pleased when one of them climbed up on the pillion seat and amidst general cries of 'tamum' 'tamum' (O.K.! O.K.!), we were directed out of the village and on down an even more indistinct cart-track. Eventually this path led us to a pleasant stream, and there our guide leapt off and plunged enthusiastically into the water with much waving of his arms. Equally suddenly it dawned on us that our beautiful weaving gestures had very understandably been mistaken for swimming motions. Our stylishly simulated woofs, warps and shuttles had been translated as a desire for a bathe to rid ourselves of the heat and dust of the road. Once again our amateurism had caught up with us, but nothing daunted we had a luxurious swim and returned to Bunyan.

Back once more in the village we were invited inside one of the little square houses, and there we understood why the carpet-making of Bunyan is so little known. Anyone coming into the village as we had done, could easily have passed right through without imagining for a moment that he was ignoring a fortune in carpets. Almost every one of the mud houses included an unusually large room which was well-lit by a long window let high up into the outer wall. In this room stood a heavy wooden loom, with the main threads running vertically and at the bottom end a large roller held by a ratchet, around which was wound the finished portion of the carpet. The hand-made construction of the loom itself can hardly have changed in a thousand years, for we learnt that carpet-making had been carried on at Bunyan long before Marco Polo passed that way. No doubt the industry of the little village is well known to the carpet dealers of Ismir, Istanbul and Kayseri, but we at least had managed to put 'the choicest and most beautiful carpets in the world' into the context which Polo had given them, and we felt that our faith in Marco's narrative and the unchanging nature of Polo's Asia had not been misplaced.

Bunyan was a living monument to the extraordinary accuracy of Marco Polo's description, and it was with growing excitement that we went from house to house eagerly examining the carpets and watching the age-old method of weaving them. Apart from the intricate carpentry, of the cunningly contrived wooden joints, beams and cross pieces in the looms without a single nail in the whole mechanism, the work of weaving a carpet was done by the women and children. While the men cultivated the fields, the rest of the family sat cross-legged on the floor before the great loom, and while daylight lasted their nimble fingers twisted and knotted the wool into place. By the side of each weaver lay a tiny pile of coloured wool ready to be woven into the carpet, and above each worker hung a piece of the pattern, done in faded squares of crayon colour on an old and tattered piece of card, though in fact it was seldom that such assistance was needed, for the designs are traditional and mainly handed down by practical experience. Even a medium-sized carpet, barely seven foot square, would take three months of assiduous effort if a woman and her two daughters worked at it over nine hours every day. With the most beautiful and intricate patterns, only the hands of children under twelve years old are nimble and supple enough to thread the delicate designs, and we could not help noticing the bent and gnarled fingers of young women whose eyesight was already failing after years of peering at their looms.

Some of the mud buildings were storehouses for the wool, which hung in thousands of shanks from the ceiling making a riot of colour which contrasted strongly with the ochres and pale yellows of the clay walls. The overall direction of the weaving was the responsibility of the village headman and the heads of the various families, though in fact the carpet buyers from the big cities had bought up Bunyan's output in good carpets for years to come. No doubt such dealers were the Armenians and Greeks whom Polo had hinted at as 'making their living by trade and commerce'. Stan, the expedition's carpet expert, was particularly struck by the fact that the patterns on the carpets were replicas of the famed Isfahan work in Persia. When he enquired further about this, we were told that this foreign design was in response to appeals from the

59

carpet dealers who could sell such patterns at a greater profit than the local patterns would fetch. So, in order that little Bunyan might be abreast of trends in far-off Persia, one of the men of the village every so often would make the long pilgrimage by whatsoever means possible to the Persian carpet-making centres where he would stand and watch the new designs being woven. Then, with the new patterns firmly imprinted on his memory, he would trek the long hard road back to Bunyan where at a village conclave he would describe what he had seen, and the new pattern books would be drawn up and distributed to the various houses.

We dearly wanted to buy a local carpet in the village, one with a real Bunyan pattern on it, but our desperate shortage of cash forbade this. Stan, however, succeeded in mysteriously separating himself from Mike and me, and just as we were getting worried about his prolonged absence, he reappeared bearing in his arms a small carpet. It was not of the finest quality, but indisputably it was of real Bunyan manufacture. Behind him strutted a small Turk, incongruously wearing one of the green jerseys, with which a kind manufacturer had provided the expedition. At the same time Stan's companion carried our small transistor radio, a donation this time from the Japanese Embassy, but a gift which had fallen silent after running out of batteries. Stan hastily explained that he had bartered the jersey and radio in straight exchange for the carpet, somewhat sheepishly adding that as his own sweater had been too large for the little Turk he had been forced to sell mine instead. Trade for trade, barter for barter, the ghost of Marco Polo must have raised a sympathetic cheer after seven centuries of silence.

The next day took us to Sivas, the town where Marco Polo says that the glorious Messer Saint Blaise suffered martyrdom, a reference to Blaise, Bishop of Sebaste in Cappadocia at the turn of the second century, who was executed under Diocletian by decapitation after being whipped and having his flesh torn by heavy iron wool combs. In Polo's day Sivas was one of the leading religious centres of the Seljuk Empire, and the city's theological colleges and mosques were renowned throughout the Muslim world. Perhaps a later Christian editor inserted the allusion to Saint Blaise to counterbalance Marco's more probable mention of Mohammedanism. But the chronicler need not have concerned himself, for little is left to mark the former glory of Sivas since the day when the hordes of Timur passed that way. The city sued for peace by sending out to the besiegers an embassy of 1000 innocent children, each one carrying before him a copy of the Koran. When Timur ordered a regiment of cavalry to crush these children beneath the hooves of their horses, the defenders of Sivas realized that there would be no quarter given and that it was the last hour of their great city. Only four thousand soldiers of the garrison were left alive when the barbarians stormed into the city. These few were all that remained of the fanatical Imperial Guard, and they died as Timur had promised, buried alive in the black earth.

Those times seem distantly savage and raw, yet in the high mountains of wilder Anatolia the peasant way of life is much the same today as it was then, or even when Xenophon's Ten Thousand suffered so harshly there. The new motor road from Sivas to Erzinjan runs straight across a flat plain, but we turned our motorcycles up along the older route through the mountains where the caravans had crawled their way between the stark peaks and ridges. Scenically the drive was really stirring, for the mineral-iferous mountains glowed in their reds, purples, greys and browns, where the naked rock lay exposed to the long winter snows and the fierce summer sun. The road itself was little more than a rough stony path along which we twisted and turned the labouring motorcycles, leaving plumes of dust along the steep climbs and round the sharp shoulders of the rocky flanks. From time to time we skidded down into valleys and the track plunged sharply into a rushing stream. Then with the engines roaring wildly, we were forced to slither crazily into the ford, hoping that our momentum would surge the machines across before water was drawn into the bubbling exhaust pipes or we came to grief on a hidden boulder.

As we drove through the isolated villages, womenfolk winnow-ing grain on the flat roofs would stop to stare at us once they had drawn their veils across the lower part of their faces. Small children ran to watch us pass. Their elder brothers eyed us from where they worked, sitting on a small board which is dragged around a central stack of corn by a pair of trotting donkeys so that the sharp runners of the sledge separate the ears of grain from the stalks. Stacks of dung lay heaped in corners ready to provide fuel for the evening cooking fires with their nostalgic, thin, pungent smell on the clear air. Through the wilder mountain villages in particular, the commotion of our passage would stir huge half-savage mastiffs wearing heavy leather collars studded with long rusty nails. These fierce hounds, ready to protect their flocks from human or wolf alike, would come bounding at us with murder in their eyes and teeth bared in snarling rage. Sitting nakedly exposed on our motorcycles, it required every effort to dodge our attackers and we learnt to carry heavy tyre levers stuck into the tops of our riding boots, so that we could club back the more vicious brutes and still keep one hand on the throttle. In this manner, high in the bleak upland, we crossed the boundary into Marco Polo's Greater Armenia.

5

MARCO POLO'S GREATER ARMENIA

Greater Armenia is a very large province. Near the entrance
to it stands a city called Erzinjan, where is made the best buckram in the world and countless other crafts are practised. Here
are the finest hot baths and natural springs to be found anywhere on earth.

THUS MARCO POLO opens his description of the eastern end
of 13th century Turkey, and goes on to say that when he visited
Erzinjan, it was the most splendid of all the towns and cities of
the province. The same can hardly be said of Erzinjan in the
present day, for although the town is still a provincial capital of
considerable local importance, it strikes the traveller as being little
more than a cross-roads on the tedious length of the main road
eastward to Persia.

At the main intersection itself the only sign of a nearby town is
a brief improvement in the decayed road surface, and down to
the right a long dusty boulevard leads to a handful of white houses
shimmering in the distant heat. The line of the Old Silk Road
beckons straight ahead for Persia, but the Marco Polo Route
Project turned aside, for we had a very special reason to visit
Erzinjan.

When Marco Polo stated that Erzinjan was famous for two
things, its 'hot baths' and 'buckram', he posed two of the most
intriguing problems which have exercised the ingenuity and
imagination of the leading experts on Polian travels. Quite

simply, these experts could not decide what on earth Marco Polo was talking about.

The mystery of the buckrams is probably the more interesting of the twin puzzles, for this word 'buckram' occurs time and again in the literature of the Middle Ages, and yet we have no precise idea of what the word means. For example, one Brother John of Plano Carpini, a Franciscan Friar, who had been sent on an embassy to the Great Khan by Pope Innocent IV in 1245, described the headgear of the Tartar womenfolk as being wooden lattice work 'covered with buckram, velvet or brocade'. Another great medieval Arab traveller, Ibn Batuta, wrote that 'At Erzinjan there are manufactured fine stuffs called after its name.' But again, by the fifteenth and sixteenth centuries the word 'buckram' was being applied to the quilted material from which doublets were made. Marco Polo himself tantalizingly uses the word on more than one occasion, so that if one could define what he meant, it might be possible to understand a little more clearly what people were weaving and wearing in the places where he travelled. At least it was obvious that Marco's 'buckram' had nothing to do with the modern word which denotes a coarse open-weave material, often of hemp, loaded with gum which is inserted as a stiffener in articles of dress. Instead, the general conclusions to be drawn from Marco Polo's ideas on buckram point to a finely worked, lustrous cloth of the highest quality, a valuable article in trade. The expedition's aim in Erzinjan was to uncover a traditional textile industry which could perhaps be traced to Polo's day and which would in turn tell us more about the mysterious buckram.

Now none of us really possessed a sufficiently comprehensive knowledge of Turkish to be able to pursue our enquiries without the aid of an interpreter, for we had learnt our lesson with the carpet miming at Bunyan. Accordingly, on reaching Erzinjan, we drove into the town and asked directions to the house of the town doctor. Here we drew a blank, for the doctor could be of little help as he depended on a knowledge of German, rather than English or French, to decipher his medical text books. Nothing daunted, we sought out the schoolmasters of Erzinjan; they at least would be fairly proficient in French, since the Turkish system of education owes much to French influence.

We found the schoolmasters congregated in the staff section of the local school, which was out on holiday, so that in fact the teachers had little to do other than sit around in their common room, drinking innumerable cups of tea and discussing the latest news gleaned from the week-old newspapers. The school was no more than a shabby single storey mud building, and the common room with its stained tables and hard wooden chairs had the atmosphere of a drab, desolate café. But due to the mutual understanding which seems to thrive between all people concerned with education, we soon struck up a sympathetic friendship with the teachers. In a way we felt sorry for the schoolmasters at Erzinjan, because in Turkey the High School staff is allocated to the various areas of the country by the central Government Ministry, and for a teacher to be sent to work in the schools of high Anatolia means exile from the more advanced cultural centres to a bleaker life in the confines of an intellectual wilderness. Nevertheless it is in schools like the one at Erzinjan that there lies the greatest field for endeavour and achievement in helping the neglected educational opportunities of the plateau people.

It must have been strange for the desperately poorly paid teachers of Erzinjan, lounging in their empty schoolhouse, to learn that people came all the way from England to visit their town in search of this strange Marco Polo. At any rate, by the time we had sketched out the problems of hot baths and buckram, we had a band of interested assistants. A conclave was called, and small boys, the ex-pupils, were sent scurrying off to summon the more intelligent and reliable of the townsfolk and cloth merchants to the discussion. Soon the room was filled with an interested gathering who sat around sipping their Çay while we all thrashed out the problem of the elusive buckram.

One of the main obstacles to our research was the fact that the old and original town of Erzinjan was totally destroyed by a tremendous earthquake in 1939. Since then the new town has been built at some distance from the ravaged site. One by one the various members of the assembly gave their opinions about the buckram, but in nearly every case their suggestions concerned modern textile weaving which could not possibly have been traced back to Polo's time. Nobody had heard of buckram or the finely woven, lustrous cloth we were looking for, until one of the schoolmasters remembered that he had a pupil whose mother, it was rumoured, carried on some sort of weaving in her home. This casual reference quickened our interest and we asked more about the family concerned. But our informant could help us no further, for he had only heard a vague report about the weaving and had himself never visited the family, as they lived on the outskirts of the town and were Armenians, not Turks. Once again the Anatolian Armenians had come into the picture and something which Polo had said about Armenians stirred in the back of my mind. I remembered that time and again Marco had cast them in the role of the artisans and craftsmen of their time. Surely this too could involve textile working. So we asked if we might not question the boy whose mother and sisters still worked at their looms.

In due course a solemn-faced child about eight or nine years old appeared before us, looking decidedly apprehensive at the surfeit of schoolmasters and the three strange Inglesi, who were so interested in him. Haltingly the lad replied to the questions of one of his teachers, and in the Turkish phrases of his answers we distinctly picked out the second half of the word 'buckram', for the boy repeatedly used the word 'ehram'.

What did the word 'ehram' mean, we asked? An ehram, we were told, is the garment which the Turkish womenfolk wrap around themselves when they leave their houses so that they are shielded from the public gaze. Of course, everywhere in Moslem communities we had seen the women swathed up like nondescript cocoons, so that very soon we took this type of dress for granted and paid no further attention to the rather dingy material which was used for their ehrams. In fact the cloth of these ehrams looked perfectly plain and more like a mass-produced factory-made article from the big cities. In all this, the teachers told us, we were perfectly correct, but the small boy who stood before us had been saying that his mother and sisters wove their own ehrams, which were the true ehrams of Erzinjan and 'were once famous among all ehrams'.

At this point a cloth merchant who had previously been silent spoke up to say that his father had always sold the ehrams of Erzinjan at a far higher price than any other sort of cloth which had been available at his stall in the bazaar. Furthermore, he himself could tell us that the ehrams of Erzinjan were unique because they derived their superfine quality from the secret

Armenian technique of weaving and the fineness of the wool which went into their making. The schoolmasters then added that for centuries the high plateau country around the town had bred a strain of sheep whose magnificent fleeces were the pride of the country people. In all Anatolia there was nowhere so blessed with good summer pasturage fed by the melting snows of the peaks. We had no reason to disbelieve them, for had not Marco Polo written of Greater Armenia that 'in the summer all the armies of the Tartars of the Levant are stationed in this province, because it has the best summer pasturage for their beasts'.

At last it seemed as if we were getting somewhere nearer the secret of the mysterious buckrams if only we could inspect one for ourselves.

Once again the helpful schoolmasters came to our aid. We were escorted to the home of the small boy's Armenian family. On the way we enquired why it was that there were so few looms left in Erzinjan, and learnt that nearly all the looms had been destroyed in the great earthquake in the old town. In all of Erzinjan there were now only half a dozen looms known to exist where the weavers worked at their ehrams, for the ancient craft was exclusive to the Armenians whose numbers had steadily dwindled since the days of bitter race hatred between Turk and Armenian. It seemed that if we had come even a few years later, or had not been so diligent in our enquiries, we would quite likely have found not the slightest trace of the ancient ehrams of Erzinjan.

As it was, we were brought to a little house built around a small courtyard, and there in one of the rooms we saw for ourselves the making of the mysterious cloth. Like the carpet looms of Bunyan, the ehram looms of Erzinjan were really ancient and occupied the best-lit room of the house. Once again, the work was carried out exclusively by the women. The cloth they wove was exactly as the Polian scholars had surmised from their studies, soft, lustrous and of the very finest quality. In shape the ehram is rather like a very delicate woollen blanket. The edges of each ehram are strengthened with a cotton hem, but the rest of the garment is made of the top-grade local wool, still brought down from the mountains by the shepherds in exchange for goods in the town market. All the ehrams came either in bleached off-white or a deep rich brown dye and their only decoration was a sprinkling of tiny red or white markings shaped like magnified snow crystals. These are called 'umbrella flowers', and nobody could explain why or how they came to be used except that for as long as the Armenians had woven ehrams they had favoured this one pattern in the making of the cloth. Most important of all, the skilled manner of the weaving and the almost translucent quality of the delicately spun wool gives each Erzinjan ehram the very special characteristic of being transparent for the person wearing it. Thus with the cloth drawn right across her face as modesty demanded, the wearer could still see out into the world around her, without in turn being seen by anyone from the outside.

Actually wearing an ehram is quite a skilled operation which the girls of Anatolia learn at an early age. The garment is draped round the body in a series of special folds which culminate in the loose end winding up from one shoulder, around the back of the head and down across the face, where it is held by the teeth so that it does not slide away to reveal the wearer's features.

When placed in a medieval context, the superfine quality and delicate weave of the cloth would obviously set it apart as a very special material. In an age more accustomed to rough homespun, the delicacy of Erzinjan buckram must have seemed very splendid and, to Marco Polo the merchant, well worth noting as an article of trade. It had even once been included in a rather sardonic royal gift when the Sheikh of the notorious Assassin sect sent a noble Crusader 'two Damascene daggers and a length of buckram to act as a winding sheet'.

Today, however, the handful of Armenian families left in Erzinjan who know the secret of the ehrams carry on their craft only out of custom and pride. For the factory-made goods turned out in the cities have displaced the far more beautiful hand-made article from the counters of the village bazaars. So there is every indication that we discovered in Erzinjan a dying art which will soon find its reference only in the works of the medieval chroniclers, as the women of Anatolia take more and more to the Western style of dress or the Armenian families forget their ancient skills.

We could not leave without first asking if it was permitted to take a photograph of the ehram being correctly worn by one of the women. But such is the strictness of the Moslem law in these areas that none of the women were willing to face the camera. Instead our original informer, the small boy, much to his embarrassment, was dressed up in an ehram by a swarm of his sisters, who in their own ehrams fluttered to and fro like ghosts, and we photographed his anonymous figure. Finally we managed to persuade the master of the house to sell one of the ehrams of Erzinjan, and so the Marco Polo Route Project added a length of buckram to the carpet we had already obtained from Bunyan.

With this accomplished, we turned our attention to the problem of the hot baths and mineral springs which Marco said could be found in the area. Rather to our disappointment none of our friends could offer us any advice, for although hot mineral springs are found all over the western end of Turkey, there is no mention of them at Erzinjan. Indeed some of the Polian scholars went so far as to say that in all likelihood Marco Polo confused Erzinjan with the town of Erzurum some distance farther along the Silk Road where there were well-known hot springs and baths. Accordingly we were almost disposed to accept this judgement but for the fact that Marco had proved himself reliable so far. Bearing this in mind, we decided to investigate the vague report that there might be some hot springs on the road to Erzurum, somewhere in the region of the earthquake site of the original Erzinjan.

Saying goodbye to all our friends and helpers in Erzinjan, we rode our motorcycles out along the Old Silk Road. After some eight miles travel the road cut across a patch of marshy ground between two stony mesas. As we rounded the flank of the first hill, the air became charged with the heavy, unmistakable smell of sulphur. This was too much to be a chance coincidence with Polo's tale, for where the earth gives forth a smell of sulphur, we might quite well find the 'finest baths and hot springs to be found anywhere on earth'. Stopping the motorcycles, we dismounted and set forth on foot into the marsh.

It was late evening and all around us the clouds of midges rose from their resting places on the sedge as we brushed our way through the reeds. The ground was like a sponge, water oozed and dripped everywhere. In our tall motorcycle boots we jumped over the quaking tussocks, the smell of the sulphur becoming stronger as we penetrated deeper into the marsh. Occasionally we stumbled across an underground stream whose roof had caved in, leaving a series of hissing, bubbling pools. We plunged our hands into the water, and tasted the drops that trickled from our fingers. Always the water was bitter and cold.

Then, quite unexpectedly, we came across a patch of higher ground, on which a mud byre had been built. Beside the hovel stood a peasant with his three water buffaloes, strange isolated denizens of the marsh. 'Ekshi Su' ('Bitter Water') we said, and he nodded, indicating that the sulphur springs were bad for his beasts. 'Sejak Su?' ('Hot Water?') we asked, and then again as he looked uncomprehendingly at us, 'Sejak Su?' Slowly he turned and raised his arm to point into the gloom, where in the last streaks of daylight over the distant chain of mountains we could just discern the silhouette of a broken-down mud building.

Thanking him, we returned to our machines and discovering a faint side track that led into the marsh we followed it by the light of our headlamps, until at length we drew up beside the building which had taken on the appearance of a small derelict temple. Then we switched off the lights and in the darkness fumbled our way into the building.

Inside the smell of sulphur was sweeter than before and somewhere we could hear the hissing and splashing of myriads of bubbles bursting upward through water. Above our heads a gaping hole in the roof let in enough starlight to enable us to make out a square black pool of water which filled the centre of the building. We lay down full length on the raised edge around the bath and plunged in our arms. To our delight, the water in the pool was warm and fizzy, a pleasant caress to the senses. That night we happily pitched our tent in the lee of this fragment of Polo's 'finest baths', and next morning when the sun awoke us, we went to inspect the pool and swim in it, as Marco Polo might have done.

The water in the pool was an unattractive turgid yellowy-brown, but once our initial hesitation was overcome we plunged in and found that the bathing was excellent. Revelling in our first wash since Istanbul, all three of us trod the clean gravel bottom of the pool, wallowing luxuriously in the warm, fizzing water as the tiny bubbles prickled deliciously up between our toes. The bath had been cunningly built over the very mineral source itself, so that the mineraliferous water welled directly up into the pool before trickling gently away through an overflow channel in one corner. Consequently, even after years of neglect, the water was perfectly clean and fresh, for it was constantly being replenished and the original designers had skilfully contrived the stonework so that any debris was automatically flushed away. We tested this for ourselves by dropping match-sticks into various parts of the pool, watching them slowly but irresistibly swirled away by the scouring currents.

The superstructure of the path was undoubtedly of recent construction, as the original building must have been destroyed in the great earthquake along with the rest of Erzinjan's baths, but the stonework and flat tiling of the pool itself dated back much further. Lounging there, in and out of the shafts of sunlight which streamed in between the polished wooden pillars which supported the roof, we felt like Roman Senators relaxing in the splendour of their own famous baths, and we could understand how for Marco such places were vividly remembered after the long weary days of plodding along the flea-bitten caravan routes.

In the end the Marco Polo Route Project spent nearly all day at the pool and it was well into the afternoon when we continued along the road to Erzurum. A few hours travelling and we were once more back among the wilder peaks and gorges of the high plateau. Driving the overloaded machines required much skill and extreme concentration, for the road zig-zagged crazily, following the contours of the mountain slopes. Under such savage conditions it was no surprise when the passenger sidecar finally gave up the unequal struggle. With a tearing rasp it half broke away from its attendant motorcycle, slewing across the track to the lip of the precipice on the outside edge. It was a very narrow escape for the rider, though the unfortunate passenger sidecar had already served us far better than we had any right to expect. Stoically it had survived collisions with Italian walls, Serbian sledge-hammers, Bulgarian kerbstones and Turkish soldiers. The last few hundred miles had been covered over the most destructive terrain only with the help of a tangled web of chains and wire, with which the weary sidecar had been strapped up to the motorcycle. There was nothing left to do but abandon our first major mechanical casualty and henceforth use one of the motorcycles as a solo machine.

That evening was one of the most miserable episodes of the

entire trip. A bitter wind sprang up in the icy peaks and swept through the defiles, cutting through our clothing and chilling us to the bone. Despite the shifting gravel surface of the track and the adjacent drop over the precipice, we had to overcome the problem of learning for the very first time how to ride a solo motorcycle without the support of a sidecar. Again and again the machine crashed over, spilling its rider onto the rocks, until Stan at last managed to master the basic technique. While he went ahead to find food, Mike and I put up the tent, battling grimly with the flapping canvas and searching the exposed mountainside for boulders to drag onto the rockflaps of the tent. By the time Stan returned, the job was done, and all three of us collapsed exhausted inside the tent, numbly scooping the greasy congealed rice from Stan's filthy crash helmet, which he had filled with nauseous food at the nearest caravanserai. We were too tired to care and huddled together for warmth as the wind shrieked over the rocks and tore at our shelter. It was small comfort to think that all this could have been nothing compared to the continued hardships which the Venetian caravan must have suffered and endured during its three and a half years of tortuous travelling.

Next day the wind had dropped, and the great leather camel bags from Istanbul's bazaar were strapped on the solo machine, which Stan rode with Mike as pillion passenger. We had already discarded any non-essential equipment, including spare machine parts, but even so the powerful 500 c.c. machine looked as grotesquely overloaded as one of the tiny donkeys trotting along wistfully beneath a mound of fodder. In this fashion we reached Erzurum, a strategic town in relation to Turkey's common frontier with the U.S.S.R., and consequently bustling with troops. But this too has hardly changed over the ages, for throughout history Erzurum has covered a strategic flank, and whether the foe was Communist, Kurd, Muslim or Persian, the garrison of Erzurum has played a key role, as the name indicates, for in Byzantine days it stood as 'the last fortified place of Rûm'.

On the other side of the town the road ran through a military zone, where we had strict instructions not to stop or leave the road. Now that we were leaving the high plateau country the countryside began to open out into wider valleys and small enclosed basins, so that it was possible to distinguish individual mountain ranges, though the general scene was still starkly barren and boulder-strewn. In all this wilderness we were on the look-out for one particular peak, Mount Ararat, for according to legend it is here that Noah's Ark came to rest and the Dove and Raven foraged.

When Ararat did at last come in sight, there was no mistaking the awesome majesty of the mountain amongst its neighbours. Nearly 17,000 feet high the snow-covered crest with its strange hump shoulder stands out strangely from the desiccated scrub of the lowland. With his usual keen perception, Marco Polo made a note of this and drew his own apt conclusions, saying that : —

> In the heart of Greater Armenia is a very high mountain, shaped like a cube, on which Noah's Ark is said to have rested, whence it is called the Mountain of Noah's Ark. It is so broad and long that it takes more than two days to go round it. On the summit the snow lies so deep all the year long that no one can ever climb it; this snow never entirely melts, but new snow is forever falling on the old, so that the level rises. But on the lower slopes, thanks to the moisture that flows down from the melting snow, the herbage is so rich and luxuriant that in summer all the beasts from near and far resort there to feed on it and yet the supply never fails.

It would hardly seem possible that such a description written at the time of the Crusades would have any relevance in an age when Mount Ararat is a forbidden military zone, from where the eye in one sweep overlooks Turkey, Russia and Persia. Yet on the slopes of the foothills below the black patch that is supposed to represent the remains of the Ark, we came across a small tribe of nomads whose existence and way of life is as old as the story of Noah itself. Every year for centuries, just as Polo had noted, the tribe had come to take advantage of the sweet summer grass fed by the meltwater of the mountain. Gradually the borders of Turkey and Persia are closing against the nomad, the Russian frontier is already blocked, yet the call of their ancient cycle still takes the dwindling bands on their migration in search of fresh pastures despite all Government pressures.

The particular group of nomads we encountered were members of that once widespread Kurdish group, which Marco insisted, perhaps from bitter personal experience, were 'lusty fighters and lawless men, very fond of robbing merchants'. But we ourselves found nothing of this and got on very well with the tribesmen who advanced from their encampment to meet us. They wore the large flat cap which is almost the clan badge of Turkish shepherds, but instead of loose jackets they had close-fitting waistcoats of gorgeously coloured velvet, picked out with curlicues of silver thread. The tribesmen clustered around us examining us no less curiously that we stared at them. In such a situation, when one wanderer meets another, some sort of understanding seems to spring up, and although we knew no word of each other's language, we were soon all sitting around the expedition's bubbling tea-making kit, sharing out cigarettes and exchanging hospitality.

The chief of the tribe was easily recognizable, for he bore an air of natural authority, and whenever he spoke the other tribesmen fell silent. Not surprisingly, the one thing which fascinated the nomads most of all was our small petrol stove, for this was the sole piece of equipment which would have been useful to them in their wandering existence. There were murmurs of approval as the tea billy came rapidly to the boil, and then we shared around the contents of the pot. With a score of drinkers, each man had only a tiny sip, but it was the gesture rather than the substance which counted, for it was obvious to the nomads that we had shared out all we had to offer and so in their turn they reciprocated the hospitality. The chieftain despatched a man to arrange for the three guests to be attended to, and one of the women herded together the wild-looking cows for milking. Soon there were set before us pannikins of delicious warm milk, bread and grapes, which were handed round as we sprawled contentedly on the cracked earth.

The scene was strikingly Biblical. The tribe's entire belongings lay scattered higgledy-piggledy upon the plain, protected by mats of peeled cane. Calves lay tethered in bunches beside the shelters, whilst the horses of the tribe trotted freely. The horses, above all, were magnificent, for they represented the wealth and luxury of their owners. Finely shaped animals, they ranged proudly without hobbles or halters, yet came in answer to their masters' call, delicate ears pricked and slim hooves mincing across the ground. Scrawny dogs and startled children darted in and out between the black tents, where there were occasional glimpses of the womenfolk.

These nomad women did not hide behind the veil but watched us demurely, brown eyes and handsome features framed in the brilliant colours, reds, oranges, purples and yellows of their fine silk scarves and shawls. Their wrists, collars and ears hung heavy with ornaments of silver, and some even wore tinkling headbands of coins dangling from curiously wrought silver chains. Wealth in horses and women's finery, homes in the tents wherever the pasture lasts, such is the nomad way of life which Polo saw along the Old Silk Road and which we too could fleetingly glimpse.

Luckily this flair of Marco Polo's for capturing a momentary picture of his surroundings is by no means restricted to observations on the local way of life. It is part of the charm of his tale that Marco is not limited to any one special interest. His agile mind darts here and there like a painter's brush, now describing a local custom, now mentioning a geographical feature. Indeed, the medieval mind knew no strict divisions into compartments of specialized knowledge, so that an artist might combine the activities of priest, general and statesman. The same scope can be seen in Marco Polo. At one moment he is describing Mount Ararat, and in the next sentence his enquiring interest is aroused by the Baku oil wells where : —

> There is a spring from which gushes a stream of oil in such abundance that a thousand camels may load there at once. The oil is not good to eat; but it is good for burning and as a salve for men and camels affected with sores.

This breadth of comment is not only a compliment to Polo's intellect, but a stroke of luck for historians. Far less would now be known about medieval Asia if Marco had merely compiled a mercantile ledger of his trading activities. As it is, his narrative provides a mine of information because Polo included all the extraneous data which he picked up along the route, scraps of history, anecdotes and legends about the lands adjacent to his path. For this reason *The Description of the World* has a much wider validity than it would otherwise possess; thus, for example, while his own story leads us through Greater Armenia, Marco pauses to tell us more about the surrounding kingdoms of Zorzania, Kurdistan, Mosul and Baghdad.

This abundance of information does however raise the difficulty that it is necessary to define which of the places he mentions Marco actually visited for himself. This is an important distinction, because we may believe Marco Polo's first-hand descriptions with far less hesitation than any hearsay accounts which he heard secondhand from other people. Obviously the only true method of deciding on Polo's true route is to visit the places concerned and test the accuracy of his statements. This test was one purpose of the Marco Polo Route Project, but before we could try out any particular route we had to sift the evidence. A major problem was the line of the Polo caravan from Ararat to the Persian Gulf.

For a great many years it was enthusiastically maintained that on leaving Greater Armenia the Polos travelled south-east into the Tigris-Euphrates depression and on to Baghdad. From there, the traditionalists believed, the family took ship and sailed down the Shatt al Arab to the Persian Gulf. This theory was based upon Marco Polo's descriptions of Mosul and Baghdad. In particular Marco gives a very fanciful account of the capture of Baghdad by Hulagu the Tartar. He describes how miserly Motassim Billah, the last of the Abbasite Caliphs, was shut up to starve in a tower full of treasure until 'after four days he died', for Hulagu said 'Now Caliph eat your fill of treasure, since you are so fond of it. For you will get nothing else?' Furthermore, Marco accurately states that Baghdad was famous for its religious colleges, its fine silks, and as the place 'where most of the pearls are pierced that are imported from India into Christendom'.

On the surface this detailed description of Baghdad seemed sufficient proof that Marco Polo actually visited the city. However, in later years another school of thought arose which supported the idea that the Polo caravan took the more obvious route eastward from Ararat to Tabriz in Armenia and then south-east along the fringe of the central Persian desert. The exponents of the latter theory pointed out that Marco only introduced the subject of Mosul and Baghdad with the words 'Now let us turn to the lands lying south and east of it (Armenia),' and that he only related facts which were common knowledge amongst Levantine middlemen. On the other hand, his description of Tabriz and Persia has a strongly personal flavour and is much more original.

This controversy was of fundamental importance in the study

of Marco Polo, for the two routes differ in places by several hundred miles. Gradually the trans-Armenian theory became the more popular, but until it could be proved that Polo visited Tabriz, there would always be some doubt. Of Tabriz Marco describes the merchant and native population a great market for precious stones, and that 'the city is entirely surrounded by attractive orchards'. The existence of the jewel market had already been corroborated by Ibn Batuta, the great fourteenth century Arab traveller, who had written : —

> In Tabriz I traversed the bazaar of the jewellers, and my eyes were dazzled by the varieties of precious stones which I beheld. Handsome slaves, superbly dressed and girded with silk, offered their gems for sale to the Tartar ladies, who bought great numbers.

There remained the question of the 'attractive orchards', about which little was known. The Marco Polo Route Project resolved to find out something more.

As it turned out, we very nearly missed the mysterious orchards, for we drove to Tabriz and found it no more than a dusty drab town with no gardens anywhere to be seen. Reluctantly we decided to give up our search and push on towards Teheran.

As we rode out of Tabriz, a silencer on one of the motorcycles dropped onto the road, and while I stayed behind to replace it, Mike wandered off until he came across a breach in the high mud wall which lined the roadway. Scrambling through the gap, he was amazed to find himself in a cool, green garden, where a Persian family sat contentedly eating a delicious picnic beneath a laden apricot tree. Mike was invited to join in the rustic feast, and soon all three of us were savouring the delicate flavour of creamy yoghourt and baby cucumbers dipped in scented syrup boiled with herbs. As far away as Abadan the cucumbers of the region are prized for their excellence, and we found ourselves eating until we could eat no more. Then we lay back on the sweet turf and stared up at the apricots hanging low over us. In such surroundings we might as well have found our way into a lesser Paradise, and after the discomforts of the road, little wonder that all the great travellers, Polo, Chardin and Abdulfeda, had remarked on the delightful gardens of Tabriz. The fortunes of the town might rise and wane, but whether it was in ancient Media, capital of Polo's Mongol Iran, or even of present day Azerbaijan, Tabriz has her gardens, fruits and orchards as a more enduring feature than all the blossomings of her political history.

'From Tabriz to Persia is twelve days' journey.' Marco continues out of Tabriz, for in his time Persia did not include Tabriz, but was the land of Fars or Persia Proper beginning at Kazvin on the Old Silk Road. The Marco Polo Route Project covered the same distance in three days, but not without incident, for one of the motorcycle front fork shafts sheared at speed, almost killing Mike, who had learnt to drive quite recklessly. As a result we had to beg a ride aboard one of the big lorries that ply the Persian roads. Loading the battered machines on board, we rumbled off towards Kazvin at a depressing twenty miles an hour.

After long hours of boredom we shook our way into Kazvin, and rolled gratefully onto the first decent arterial road since Ankara. About 100 miles ahead lay Teheran, and while Stan went on by lorry to the capital with the crippled bike, Mike and I took the useable solo machine for a flying visit to the legendary Valley of the Assassins.

6

VALLEY OF THE ASSASSINS

THE RISE AND FALL of the power of the Assassins is one of the
most extraordinary phenomena of the Middle Ages. In the space
of a few years the fanatical followers of the Old Man of the
Mountains made the word 'Assassin' feared throughout the length
and breadth of the known world. Yet the Assassin kingdom itself
lasted for only little more than a hundred years before it fell to the
all-conquering hordes of Tartars. The founder of the Assassins
was an adventurer by the name of Hassan ben Sabbah, who in
about 1090 was exiled from the Persian court during the reign of
Malik Shah Jelal-eddin, third sovereign of the Seljukian dynasty.
Fleeing from the capital under sentence of death, Hassan Sabbah
took refuge in the grim tangle of the Elburz mountains, which
stretch in a great arc around the southern end of the Caspian
Sea.

Whilst wandering with his tiny band of retainers in these inhospitable mountains, Hassan Sabbah stumbled across the Assassin
valley—a huge fertile gash in the very heart of the sierras, which
soar upward like jagged ramparts on every side of the hidden
valley. Only three narrow tracks threaded their way into the secret
lair, and these paths could be held by a few men against an
entire army. Chance had presented him with a freak of nature,
which Hassan Sabbah could turn into a tiny fortified kingdom,
where he could raise the standard of rebellion against the Imperial power. Soon his camp attracted scores of other outlaws who

were sworn into his following. As his forces swelled, so Hassan Sabbah took upon himself the title of Sheik el Jebel, or Lord of the Mountains, proclaiming that he was Chosen of Allah and would lead his people back to the strict path of the True Belief.

This pattern of revolt was really nothing very unusual for the turbulent times of the Middle Ages, and it is quite possible that the Assassins would have continued to plunder and pillage in the customary manner of common mountain brigands, until a major Imperial expedition wiped out their nest. But Hassan Sabbah was no ordinary man, and his talk of the Faith inspired his followers to believe that their Sheik was indeed one of the Prophets, who held the gift of immortality for the faithful. Sabbah welded these fanatics into the most effective system of political killers that the world has ever known, and by skilful use of this unparalleled murder weapon the Sheik el Jebel was able to strike at the very head of any power which dared confront him. In Asia and Europe every ruler came to know by example that his life lay in danger of sudden death with dagger, poison or garrotte. Soon, not only did the Old Man of the Mountain send out executioners on his own errands, but Assassins were hired out to other potentates who schemed against their fellows. Prince Edward of England, Louis IX and Emperor Frederick II all narrowly escaped death at the hands of Assassin emissaries. The Prince of Homs and the Prince of Mosul were murdered in their own mosques by Assassins, and even in far Mongolia the Khakhan Mangu, surrounded by a picked bodyguard of 500 men, was forced to take refuge in his tent, when the rumour spread that a hundred disguised Assassins had infiltrated into the Royal encampment on their mission of death.

Although further branches of the Assassins sprang up in the wild mountainous area of other Middle Eastern countries, the original centre in the Elburz ranges remained the foremost of the Assassin strongholds, extending its sway over much of the surrounding countryside, including the town of Kazvin at the foot of the mountain chain. Time and again the Imperial rulers launched expeditions against the upstart Assassins, who sacked the rich towns of the lowlands and ambushed the slow-moving caravans. But always the impregnable castles of the Assassins, set like eagles' nests amongst the high peaks, withstood the most determined sieges, whilst the attacking forces were constantly exposed to the threat of violent deaths amongst their leaders.

The fanaticism of the Assassins' devotion towards their chieftains was legendary. On one occasion a noble Crusader, Henry Count of Champagne, titular king of Jerusalem, was invited to visit an Assassin fortress in Syria. As his host led him around the ramparts, the two leaders discussed the importance of personal devotion from their retainers. To illustrate that he could command instant and absolute obedience, the Assassin Sheik turned towards a group of his 'fidawi' or fanatic followers, who were standing idly on a nearby tower, and with a wave of his arm the Sheik gestured that they should leap from the walls. Unhesitatingly the young men obeyed and jumped straight to their deaths on the rocks far below.

So powerful was the influence of the Assassins that the Great Khan of the Mongols sent a Chinese general to spy out their position. When Hulagu Khan invaded Persia, one of his express intentions was to wipe out the sect, which by then held 360 fortified places in the Elburz mountains alone, and maintained an army of sturdy youths. The Assassins knew that their days were numbered, and the Grand Master of the Order sent word to the European courts, asking for help against their common Tartar enemy. But Europe was only too pleased that the Assassins had at last met their match, and in the words of the Bishop of Winchester, the cold reply returned 'Let Dog eat Dog'.

In 1256 the Assassins were finally swept away when the torrent of Tartars swamped them by sheer weight of numbers. Hulagu, at the head of his vast army and assisted by his famous generals Baidu and the Naiman Kitbuka, a Christian Nestorian from Mongolia, passed over the Elburz mountains like a tidal wave. The hordes of Tartars lapped around the foothills, and reduced the fortresses one by one. With only a few outposts left uncaptured, Hulagu surged on to Baghdad, leaving behind small detachments to hold down the shattered fragments of the Assassin forces. One such garrison was to hold out for no less than fourteen years of siege, and in the end they surrendered not from starvation, but from lack of clothing.

By the time Marco Polo's caravan journeyed through Kazvin and wound its way past the flanks of the forbidding Elburz mountains, the power of the Assassins had already been smashed by the Tartars, and the caravans could travel in safety by special order of the Mongol Ilkhan. But the legend of the dreaded Assassins still survived, and tales of the strange mountain fanatics lingered on around the evening campfires. The word 'Assassin' is supposed to be derived from 'hashish' with which the Old Man of the Mountain used to drug his novices, and in the thirteenth century when Marco visited Persia, the memory of the Assassin kingdom was so fresh that, although he never visited it for himself, Marco wrote the most famous and probably the finest description ever made of the mysterious valley : —

He (the Old Man of the Mountains) caused to be made in a valley between two mountains the biggest and most beautiful garden that was ever seen, ornamented with gold and with likenesses of all that is beautiful on earth, and also four conduits, one flowing with wine, one with milk, one with honey, and one with water. Fair ladies were there and damsels, the loveliest in the world, unsurpassed at playing every sort of instrument and at singing and dancing. And he gave his men to understand that this garden was Paradise. That is why he made it after this pattern, because Mahomet assured the Saracens that those who go to Paradise will have beautiful women to their heart's content to do their bidding and will find there rivers of wine and milk and honey and water. So he ordered this garden made like the Paradise that Mahomet promised to the Saracens, and the Saracens of this country believed that it really was Paradise. No one ever entered this garden except those whom he wished to make Assassins. At the entrance stood a castle so strong that it need not fear any man in the world, and there was no way in except through this castle. The Sheik kept with him at his court all the youths of the country from twelve years old to twenty, all, that is, who shaped well as men at arms. These youths knew well by hearsay that Mahomet their prophet had declared Paradise to be made in such a fashion as I have described, and so they accepted it as truth. Now mark what follows. He used to put some of these youths in this Paradise, four at a time, or ten, or twenty, according as he wished. And this is how he did it. He would give them draughts that sent them to sleep immediately. Then he had them taken and put into the garden, where they were wakened. When they awoke and found themselves in there and saw all the things I told you of, they believed that they really were in Paradise. And the ladies and the damsels stayed with them all the time, singing and making music for their delight and ministering to all their desires. So these youths had all that they wished for and asked nothing better than to remain there.

Now the Sheik held his court with great splendour and magnificence and bore himself most nobly and convinced the simple mountain folk that were around him that he was a prophet; and they believed it to be the truth. And when he wanted emissaries to send on some mission of murder, he would administer the drug to as many as he pleased; and while they slept he had them carried into his palace. When these youths awoke and found themselves within the castle, they were amazed and were by no means glad, for the Paradise from which they had come was not a place that they would ever willingly have left. They went forthwith to the Sheik and humbled themselves before him, as men who believed that he was a great prophet. When he asked them whence they came, they would answer that they had come from Paradise, and that this was in truth the Paradise of which Mahomet had told their ancestors; and they would tell their listeners all that they had found there. And others who heard this and had not been there were filled with a great longing to go to this Paradise; they longed for death so that they might go there, and looked forward eagerly to the day of their going.

When the Sheik desired the death of some great Lord, he would first try an experiment to find out which of his Assassins was the best. He would send some of them off on a mission in the neighbourhood at no great distance with orders to kill such and such a man. They went without demur and did the bidding of their Lord. Then, when they had killed the man, they returned to court—those of them that escaped, for some were caught and put to death. When they had returned to their lord and had told him that they had faithfully performed their task, the Sheik would make a great feast in their honour. And he knew very well which of them had displayed the greatest zeal, because after each he had sent other of his men as spies to report which was the most daring and the best hand at murdering. Then, in order to bring about the death of the lord or other man which he desired, he would take some of these Assassins of his and send them wherever he might wish, telling them that he was minded to dispatch them to Paradise; they would go

Valley of the Assassins

accordingly and kill such and such a man; if they died on their mission, they would go there all the sooner. Those who received such a command obeyed it with a right good will, more readily than anything else they might have been called on to do. Away they went and did all they were commanded. Thus it happened that no one ever escaped when the Sheik of the Mountain desired his death.

As it happened, it had never been part of the Marco Polo Route Project that we should visit the fabulous hidden valley. But Marco's description was so enticing that Mike and I decided on the spur of the moment to explore the valley, while the damaged motorcycle was being repaired in Teheran. What we did not realize was the magnitude of the undertaking. We were not to know that a visitor intruding on this valley normally went only after careful preparation, making sure that they had excellent maps and adequate food, for the mountains are wild, desolate places which do not welcome the unprepared stranger. When we set out, all we took with us was a copy of Marco Polo's book and the camera equipment. We blithely supposed that the trip would take little more than an afternoon, and so allowed ourselves only a few shillings of Persian money.

Our first step was to ask in Kazvin how to find the path to the secret valley. Marco Polo calls the place 'Mulehet', which can be translated as the plural of the Persian word for heretic, and we were told in Kazvin that the place of the heretics was the Valley called Alimut, (a contraction of Mulihedet-ul-Maut—the Heretics of Death). The key to finding the valley in the tangle of mountains is to select the correct track which branches off the main Teheran road out of Kazvin. For hours we chugged up and down this road on our motorcycle, asking at the chay khanehs about the Alimut. By the time we located the track we sought, it was late in the evening, so we spent the night at a small and rather rough-looking caravanserai, where we dragged the bike into the sleeping room with us for fear of thieves. Next morning we bumped our way across the rough, dusty track, heading into the first swells of the foothills.

Today the Elburz mountains are still as grim and forbidding as they must have been when Hassan Sabbah fled there for refuge. It was not easy to penetrate into them along the narrow mule

84

track, and to add to our difficulties it was the first time that I had ever ridden a solo motorcycle, with or without a pillion passenger.

The sudden change from the flat plains to the rocky mountain slopes was remarkable. One moment we were negotiating small pot-holes and dried-up ditches on the lowland, and the next instant we found ourselves changing down to bottom gear and grinding up between scree-covered cliffs. The desolation was extraordinary; nothing moved or made a sound in those hills; only the grey and blistered cliffs re-echoed the laboured roar of our machine as we climbed higher and higher.

On a motorcycle the ascent was terrifying, and it would have been no easy matter on muleback. Mike kept admirably silent, whatever he must have felt like as the machine wobbled its way around the loops in the slender track. The surface of the path was covered with a treacherously loose carpet of rock fragments, and these scrunched and slipped beneath the worn tyres. The track hugged the shoulders of the mountainside and usually we clawed our way along with a thousand foot drop on the outside lip. At one point we could not help noticing the burnt-out wreckage of a jeep which had obviously slid over the edge, and now lay like a smashed toy with its gutted underside turned upward.

Now and again we stopped to gather our strength for the next part of the ascent, talking as if the Alimut lay just over the skyline. Yet always there was another ridge and yet another crest, as we surmounted the last one. After hours of tortuous progress across several of the main ridges, we found ourselves churning upward into the cloud that obscured the higher peaks. Now movement was really dangerous, for the surging mist reduced visibility to a few yards, and the soft caress of the cloud turned the shifting surface of the path into a glassy rock slide. The track sloped noticeably downwards across its width, so that every time the bike tipped over, we slid dangerously towards the chasm on the outside shoulder. Whenever this happened, we scrabbled furiously to prevent ourselves from slipping over the precipice; the stones we dislodged clattering outward into the mist and, after a long silence, smashing down onto the unseen rocks far below.

Well into the afternoon, the path at last began to descend. And then, quite suddenly, we emerged from underneath the cloud and stopped in amazement at the view spread out before us. Dropping away almost sheer beneath our feet and bathed in brilliant sunshine lay the deep cleft of a river valley. In the cleft ran the tiny silver thread of a river slicing its way through the heart of the mountains. On the other side of the river rose up the almost vertical wall of a great razor-topped ridge. This barrier stood like some gigantic castle rampart, a huge reef of rock running directly across our path. Over the ridge, we looked down onto a sea of white clouds pooled between the encircling mountains. These clouds hung like a canopy over the secret valley so that no one could look down into it from the other peaks. Later we also learnt that the clouds supplied the valley with daily rain showers, making it flourish like a green Paradise amidst the dismal highlands.

The flank of the final barrier ridge was an awesome sight. Towering above the Alimut river, it dwarfed the water-course until it seemed no larger than a tiny rivulet. The rock face rose up in a dazzling swirl of colours. The mountain wall glowed with reds, greens, greys, browns and blues of every shade and hue. By some freak of stratigraphy, the different rock-bands had weathered into a thousand colours that mingled and emerged in streaks and patches, as if some artistic Titan had used the cliff for a palette on which to mix his paints.

Quickly we rode down to the river. The path coiled down in a series of heart-stopping swoops, till it ran out level along the bank of the Alimut river, which turned out to be a rushing torrent of clear, cold mountain water. A quarter of a mile downstream, the track ended abruptly at an idyllic caravanserai, around which were tethered a dozen mules. On the bank grew a huge tree, and in the shade of its enormous spread of branches was a raised table of earth, against which sprawled the muleteers, eating flat unleavened bread dipped in bowls of creamy yoghourt. The owner of the caravanserai came forward to welcome us, and we collapsed gratefully on the carpets he spread on the ground. After the trials of our journey, we both sat quietly for some time, gratefully enjoying the cool calm of the rest-house.

Turning to a muleteer, we asked :

'Which way to the Alimut and the Castle of Hassan Sabbah?'

The mule-driver raised his arm and pointed across the river, 'That is the way to the Alimut, but your motor machine cannot go there with you, for the river is deep and dangerous in this season.'

'How then are we able to reach the Assassin castle?' we enquired.

'The best way is by mule-train for you and your equipment,' came the reply.

'That would be too expensive for us, and besides we bring no equipment. We will enter alone and on foot.'

So saying, we rose to leave. First we said goodbye to our host, who would accept no payment for the food he had provided. Furthermore, he promised to look after our motorcycle while we were away. Then, followed by the astonished looks of the mule-teers who could not believe that we were really set on entering the Assassin valley alone, we continued downstream on foot for a few hundred yards until the main river disappeared between the tall cliffs that closed in from either side. On the opposite bank, the Alimut river was joined by a smaller tributary that cut directly across the ridge of many colours. This tributary sliced its way through a narrow, winding gorge, which opened like a slender knife-thrust in the flank of the mountain. This was the entrance to the Hidden Paradise. Very gingerly, we stepped into the main river and began to inch our way across the swirling torrent. A line of half-submerged boulders marked the route of the ford, and we felt our way anxiously between these beacons, holding our camera gear high in the air. As we drew closer to the gorge on the other side, the going became even harder, for the tributary river shot out powerfully, so that it was as much as we could do to keep our footing on the river bed. The water foamed around our chests as we gradually forced ourselves against the pressure of the stream into the ravine opposite. Above our heads, the yellow sand-stone walls of the gorge soared on upward, and in front of us the river came boiling around the rock buttresses as the channel twisted its tortured way through the mountain barrier.

At one point Mike, a few yards in the lead, was picked up bodily by a moving whirl-pool, and carried fifteen yards downstream, pirouetting gracefully but helplessly like a floating ballet dancer, his precious cine camera held high above his head. A little farther on, we came to a shoal where it was possible to stand comfortably and Mike asked me to ford out into the stream, so that he could film the difficulties of entering the Assassin valley. Boldly I complied, and stepped straight into a good six feet of rushing water, disappearing completely in the most realistic style that any cameraman could possibly have demanded.

Straining our way into the gorge, it was easy to understand how difficult it was to find the secret valley, and also how well defended was the Assassins' lair. To enter the raging torrent in the gorge seemed madness in the first instance, but to attempt it in the face of determined defenders would be well-nigh impossible. Yet on the other side of the ravine, one walks out quite suddenly onto the broad, flat floor of a fertile valley. The sides of the valley rise up steeply, but cradled between them is a land-locked Paradise. On the other side of the gorge the mountains had been bare and harsh, here in the Alimut our ears were filled with the gurgling and splashing of the hundreds of little runnels which Marco Polo had mentioned. In a land crippled by the scarcity of water, it is no wonder that the wretched mountain tribes, ekeing out a miserable existence on the dry upland slopes, rumoured of a hidden Paradise which flowed with milk and honey. In the valley, a myriad of little streams and water-courses babbled their criss-cross paths over the ground. Willows, sedge and bull-rushes indicated the line of the larger streams, and on all sides grew lush grass or crops of rice, interspersed with clumps of trees.

Not seeing any houses or people working in the fields, we walked on up the valley. Without a guide and not knowing the best trails, we found ourselves fording more water channels or squelching our way knee-deep in mud across the paddy fields. Our earlier hardships with the river and motorcycle had exhausted us, so we were more than glad to blunder across a villainous-looking muleteer, watering two of his beasts in one of the streams. Dumping the camera gear on the ground, we squatted next to him and began the long haggle over the price of our ride.

'Salaam alik! Can you take us to the Alimut castle?' we asked.

'It is two days journey, and I go to the gorge,' was the reply.

'But how much will it cost for you to take us to the castle of Hassan Sabbah,' we ventured.

'At least forty tuman per person and the price of a night's lodging for my beasts and I,' answered the muleteer.

'That is too much, we are very poor.'

'No one of your colour and race is poor,' was the surly response.

Eventually we beat down the price to three tuman each plus the night's lodging, though this required at least an hour's bartering and some realistic play-acting at getting up and leaving the discussion altogether, though in fact neither of us was in a fit state to continue much farther on foot. Loading the cameras into the mule bags which hung across the animals backs, we climbed aboard, and with the muleteer striding along behind, pushed deeper into the mysterious valley of the Assassins on our way to the famous Alimut Rock, on which the Old Man of the Mountain had built his castle stronghold, the Eagle's Nest.

Travelling by mule turned out to be a great improvement on walking, though it was remarkable how easily the mule-driver kept up with his beasts. Perhaps this was just as well, for Mike was regaining his normal high spirits and began his usual clowning. The comparison between the Assassin valley and the more spectacular Hollywood Westerns was too much for him, and soon the sierras rang with the time-worn film phrases about 'a place big enough for a man to breathe in, fit to build schools, churches and bring up our families'. Eventually the long-suffering mule could stand it no longer and suddenly raced off, so that the Hollywood hero was forced to cling inelegantly around its neck with a muffled flood of East End expletives. After a hectic chase the muleteer caught up with his charge, and thenceforth insisted on leading the animal himself, despite Mike's wheedling entreaties to 'please give him back his reins as he promised to be out of town by sun-down'.

We rode all afternoon, squelching across the soggy valley floor or following the path which climbed up the side of the valley so that once more we were shrouded in the low clouds. Whenever the mist closed in around us, the guide would give voice to a long, doleful dirge to quiet the anxieties of his animals, which minced delicately through the clammy whiteness. Occasionally we heard the sound of a muleteer's song coming towards us, and suddenly out of the mist ahead would loom the indistinct shapes of other mule-trains, and the two groups would shuffle gingerly past each other on the narrow track. Excited questions flew back and forth, as the newcomers asked about the two strange visitors to the valley, who had wandered through the gorge by themselves, and the curious mules looked up at us from under the fringes of lucky blue beads which decorated their bridles.

As the day wore on and darkness fell, it became obvious that our little party would not reach the village of the Eagle's Nest that night. So we groped our way through the pitch black towards the lights of a little village that glimmered below us on the floor of the valley. Descending the slope, the mules were very tired and stumbled frequently, whilst the surly muleteer cursed in the dark behind us and began demanding higher wages for his journey. Mike and I sat hunched in our saddles and wondered what lay ahead.

In the village we made our way from house to house, seeking shelter for ourselves and stabling for the mules. When hope was almost gone, we found a place to take us in, and we bedded down the animals in the byre, before limping gratefully into the warmth of the communal living room. There we were given food and a carpet to sleep on, whilst our guide sulked blackly in one corner and refused to eat with us, eating alone in sullen silence. The owners of the house were not so unfriendly, and soon we were answering a barrage of questions about ourselves and the way we had come, for there were few people who had ever ventured out of the gorge and seen the world beyond the Assassin valley.

Finally the menfolk grew weary, the giggling group of women against the far wall faded away, and all of us rolled up in our rugs on the floor to get some rest. But for Mike and I sleep did not come easily. The blankets had only just been taken from the mules and they crawled with vermin of every kind and size. The humid atmosphere of the rainy valley encouraged legions of ravenous insect life, and the lush paddies were flourishing breeding grounds for malarial mosquitoes. All that night we tossed and turned under the searing fire of bites. The floor of the communal room literally seethed with bugs which appeared from the cracks in the mud floor, and when one struck a match, the sudden flare would clear an empty space in the pool of light, while the insects fought to pack deeper in the dark corners.

After breakfast we were eager to be on our way, when out of the blue the muleteer refused to go any farther and demanded his money. We insisted that first we would pay the landlord for his hospitality. But, in paying our host, we found that our night's lodging had cost us all the money we had brought with us. This, however, was not so easy to explain to the muleteer, who had already started the day in a great rage. He violently refused to believe that any European could really and truly be without money. As he stormed and ranted, there was nothing we could do to calm him. We promised to send him his money from Teheran, but he would not hear of it. We suggested payment in kind; he could have sheath knives, dark glasses or what he would. Such things were worth far more than the few shillings of our fare on his mules, but he was not to be appeased. In a paroxysm of anger he was determined to be difficult and even attempted to search us for hidden coins. Then suddenly, with a heated insult, he grabbed Mike's precious movie camera and began to make off with it. This was the final blow to our frayed patience. Without a word between us, Mike and I sprang on the muleteer in calculated fury. The ensuing brawl was very brief, for our adversary had obviously never bargained that Europeans were willing to indulge in what Mike lovingly calls a 'punch-up'. A few wild blows, and the whole affair was over. The mule-driver lay in the mud, and Mike was once again in possession of his camera equipment.

Unfortunately, the unprecedented spectacle of two destitute Europeans brawling with a muleteer created an explosive atmosphere in the village. The situation called for quick action, so we appealed to the village headman to settle our dispute. The headman, in turn, called together the council of village elders, which congregated in the village square to sit in judgement. As the sun rose higher, the long arguments flew back and forth. For our own part, Mike and I mostly kept silent; anything else seemed a waste of breath and anyhow our Persian vocabulary was severely limited in such situation. By mid-day the court was still in full spate, though by then it seemed as if we were winning our case, after it had been explained that in truth we had no money left after paying for the night's stay. The council accepted that we had tried our best to give presents in place of money, and that these had been refused. Then, one by one, began the harangues against our surly muleteer, until Mike and I began to feel quite sorry for him. It appeared that in the first place mulemen are held in low esteem by villagers. Furthermore, this particular muleteer came from another village and had a bad reputation. To clinch the argument, it was proved that when we had met him the muleteer had in· fact been going our way already, so that to pay him at all for his two miserable beasts was an act of charity.

When all the talking had exhausted itself, the headman gave sentence. The muleteer was ordered to leave the village at once and be thankful for a free night's food and lodging for himself and his animals. Then the headman turned to us, and with a courteous wave of his hand apologized for the misfortune that had befallen us in his village. From that moment we were to consider ourselves as guests under his protection.

We set out on the last leg of our journey to the castle of Hassan Sabbah. This time we travelled on foot with a strong escort of village elders, and every so often, the little procession halted, as one of the men turned back to the village, but not before he had ceremoniously embraced us farewell, a prickly process involving his bushy beard. At last, only the headman and his small son were left, and the two of them insisted on carrying all our equipment. At length we were brought to a rickety bridge built of rough tree-trunks laid across the racing waters of the main river, and there the old man removed his felt skull-cap, dipped it in the stream, and offered us a drink from it—the final courtesy to a departing traveller. At the river, the headman told us, his authority and the land of his village ended, but on the other side we would find a group from the next village waiting to receive us and take us on our journey. Thus we were passed from settlement to settlement with great kindness and many ceremonial cups of tea, until we reached the village that nestles under the great bulk of the Alimut Rock on which the Eagle's Nest is built.

As we struggled up the steep slope leading to the final village, a small boy came running to tell us that there was an 'Americani' staying at the house of the headman. Curiously we followed him to the big central house, and there we found our mysterious American, resplendent in battle-dress and surrounded by hygenic containers of food and water brought specially from Teheran. His superbly equipped mule train was stabled nearby under the care of two bodyguards, and his interpreter fondled a fierce-looking shotgun. Faced with this display of lavish professionalism, we could not resist the opportunity of flaunting a mild attitude of irresponsibility. In response to his questions, we casually mentioned that we had come up the Assassin's valley for a pleasant stroll encouraged by a mere tourist's whim, and followed up by trying to look nonchalantly unconcerned at the American's tales of fierce wolves which roamed the valley after nightfall. Having thus unfairly gained the upper hand, it was easy to borrow some very badly needed money from our new found acquaintance before the headman sent us up the path to the Eagle's Nest, guided by two retainers.

The final climb into the castle we had come to see was the most exhausting phase of our journey. The castle is built on the flat crown of a gigantic sandstone boulder which juts out from the cliffside of the valley like the prow of an enormous ship. The only access to the top of the Alimut Rock is along the thread of a narrow path which snakes its way up the face of the cliff, before running into the cleft between the Rock and the mountain. Toiling along this path, we were like puny ants threatened by a rock which loomed over us, poised as if to obliterate anyone who dared approach.

Today, there is very little left of the fortress structure on top of the Alimut Rock. All that remain are a few rather disappointing stumps of dry stone walls, for, when the Mongols captured the Alimut, Khan Hulagu ordered that any fortifications should be razed to the ground, so that never again would the evil Assassin sect flourish in the hidden valley. But concealed in the bulk of the Alimut Rock survive two small caves, which had been hollowed out with chisels, and in these caves, by some quirk of geology, were little pools of drinkable water. Without these pools the Rock would have been untenable, but because of this indispensable water supply the fortress had succeeded in holding out against the Tartars over four long years of siege, whilst attacker and defender had struggled in hand-to-hand combat on the narrow path amidst a shower of Assassin boulders and Mongol arrows.

Although so little remains of the castle, the atmosphere of the notorious Eagle's Nest cannot have changed much since Hassan Sabbah ruled there. Perched up as if in space, a sheer drop on every side, one can look out just as once the Assassin chiefs looked out. Far below spreads the green fertility of the hidden valley, dotted with the occasional clumps of trees that surround the miniature Assassin villages. The cloud-shadows chase each other across the fields divided by the glitter of sunlight on the streamlets, and always bounding every horizon rise the grey mountain peaks half hidden in cloud, where once the Assassin sentinels kept watch over the secret of the valley, concealed amid the apparently unbroken desolation of the Elburz ranges.

Now the peaks are inhabited only by shepherd boys watching over their flocks of horned sheep and goats. From where we stood on the crest of the great Rock, we could see one such shepherd on a nearby crag. He was only a few hundred feet away, but between us gaped a thousand foot chasm. In the still air it was possible to distinguish every detail of his dress, and the clink of his staff on the pebbles floated clearly across to us. One of our guides beckoned him over, and the youth left his flock and began to run full tilt down the precipitous slope of shale. The slithering figure seemed to be dashing to a certain death on the appalling slope, yet somehow the boy maintained his balance and, dropping nimbly down to the bottom of the cliff, scrambled up the face of the Alimut Rock. In an unbelievably short space of time he stood before us, scarcely panting after his climb, which had taken Mike and I a good half-hour of steady effort. In one hand the boy carried a staff which he used as a balancing pole, and unlike the barefoot children of the lowland he wore stout sandals of leather with thick soles, onto which were nailed small horse-shoes of iron to steady his footing on the rough terrain. It was not difficult to discern in him the wiry, proud descendant of the fierce Assassin 'fidawi', who had managed to slay Ahmed Yel, Prince of Maragha, at Baghdad in the presence of his Almighty Omnipotence, Mahomed Grand Sultan of Persia.

The two of us spent the following night in the village at the foot of the Rock, and at daybreak we walked back to the floor of the valley. There we encountered a mule train on its way to the gorge, and rode with them to the lovely caravanserai on the other side. By strange coincidence, we ran across our original, surly muleteer waiting at the gorge, and were able to pay him with the money borrowed from our American friend. The unfortunate muleteer could hardly believe his eyes as he saw the notes pressed into his hand, and we did not enlighten him as to the mystery of our new-found wealth. That, we decided, would be one more secret about the strange valley.

Collecting our motorcycle from the caravanserai, we started out on the long and difficult road back over the mountains. By now, neither of us had slept or eaten well for three days. We were so exhausted that in the first five miles the bike toppled over more than thirty times. Then, disastrously, in one particular jarring crash the machine trapped my right leg against a boulder, smashing some of the bones in the foot. Luckily the heavy motorcycle boot saved the worst of the damage, but our situation was unenviable, for Mike had not yet learned to ride the bike solo, and I was effectively crippled. With characteristic ingenuity Mike managed to arrange at a small Assassin settlement for our machine to be looked after, and we prepared to limp out over the mountains. But our good fortune had not entirely deserted us, for we had not gone far, when we heard the sound of a jeep nosing its way along the track. Our saviours turned out to be a small team of copper prospectors, surveying the wild area by some remote chance which led them to the scene of our crash. Very kindly they took us back to the main road, where we managed to hitch-hike to a cheap hotel in Teheran, arriving in the early hours of the morning.

7

THE VILLAGE OF THE MAGI

THE INJURY TO MY FOOT completely disrupted the plans of
the Marco Polo Route Project. Washed, shaved, injected, X-rayed,
disinfected and with my foot in plaster, I welcomed the other two
to the luxurious oil company nursing home where I was laid up.
Stan and Mike had done their own recuperating under the influence of a private swimming pool and gin, supplied through the
generous hospitality of the Teheran manager of Richard Costain Ltd. The second sidecar had been abandoned, as it was also
showing signs of strain, but the two motorcycles were once more
roadworthy. The Marco Polo Route Project held a Council of
War, and decided that we should have to split forces. The doctor
had assured me that my foot would be out of action for at least
two months, so motorcycling was impossible for me. Therefore
Stan and Mike would take the two bikes and push on in a great
Easterly sweep through Isfahan, Kirman and Kandahar to Kabul.
I was to follow on as best I could, my task being to investigate
Polo's highly controversial route in Southern Persia and Northern
Afghanistan.

As soon as this arrangement had been decided, Mike and Stan
left on their journey. Their first objective was a small village called
Aveh, which lies about 100 miles to the south-west of Teheran.
To the inhabitants of the area there is nothing very special about
Aveh. It is simply another village hidden in the barren plateau.
But Marco Polo states quite categorically that Aveh was no less

96

The Village of the Magi

than the home of one of the Three Wise Men, and that from this particular corner of the Great Salt Steppe, the Magi journeyed to far Bethlehem. According to Marco;

In Persia there is a city called Saveh, from which the three Magi set out when they came to worship Jesus Christ. Here, too, they lie buried in three sepulchres of great size and beauty. Above each sepulchre is a square building with a domed roof of very fine workmanship. The one just beside the other. Their bodies are still whole, and they have hair and beards. One was named Balthazar, the second Gaspar, and the third Melchior. Messer Marco asked several of the inhabitants who these Magi were; but no one could tell him anything except that they were three kings who were buried there in days gone by. But at last he learnt what I will tell you.

Three days further on he found a town called Kala Atishparastan, the inhabitants of which declare that in bygone days the three kings of this country went to worship a new-born prophet and took with them three offerings—gold, frankincense, and myrrh—so as to discover whether this prophet was a god, or an earthly king, or a healer. For they said : 'If he takes gold, he is an earthly king; if frankincense, a god; if myrrh, a healer.' When they had come to the place where the prophet was born, the youngest of the three kings went in all alone to see the child. He found that he was like himself, to wit of his own age and appearance. And he came out, full of wonder. Then in went the second, who was a man of middle age. And to him also the child seemed, as it had seemed to the other, to be of his own age and appearance. And he came out quite dumbfounded. Then in went the third, who was of riper years; and to him also it happened as to the other two. And he came out in deep thought. When the three kings were all together, each told the others what he had seen. And they were much amazed and resolved that they would all go in together. So in they went, all three together, and came before the child and saw him in his real likeness and in his real age; namely only thirteen days old. Then they worshipped him and offered him the gold, the frankincense and myrrh. The child took all three offerings and then gave them a closed casket. And the three kings set out to return to their own country.... Let me tell you finally that one of the three Magi came from Saveh, one from Aveh and one from Kala Atishparastan.

97

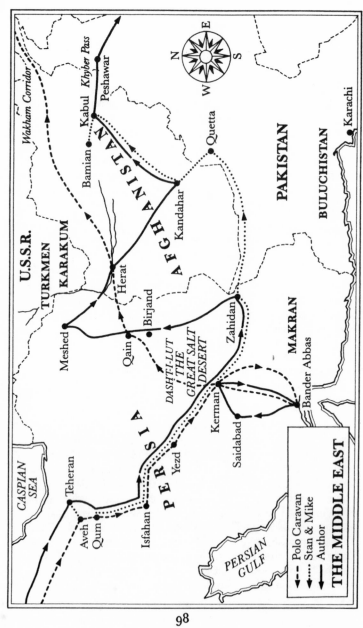

CASPIAN SEA

U.S.S.R.

TURKMEN

KARAKUM

Wakham Corridor

Khyber Pass

Peshawar

Kabul

Bamian

A F G H A N I S T A N

Quetta

Kandahar

PAKISTAN

BULUCHISTAN

Karachi

Meshed

Herat

Qain

Birjand

DASHT-I-LUT
THE
GREAT SALT
DESERT

Zahidan

MAKRAN

Teheran

Aveh

Qum

Isfahan

Yezd

P E R S I A

Kerman

Saidabad

Bander Abbas

PERSIAN
GULF

- - - Polo Caravan
······ Stan & Mike
——— Author

THE MIDDLE EAST

98

Of these three settlements, Aveh was selected for the expedition's visit, because it was the most remote of the trio and there was no record that it had been visited by anyone interested in the Magi. In fact, so little was known about Aveh that of two scholarly authorities one placed the village sixteen miles S.S.E. of Saveh, and the other expert insisted that Aveh really lay sixty miles in the opposite direction. In all this muddle Mike and Stan were not expecting to find any conclusive proof that one of the Magi had definitely come from Aveh; this would have been far too optimistic when there is hardly an ancient city of the East that does not vehemently claim this distinction. The purpose of their visit was to search out some evidence that might still link the present settlement at Aveh with the days of the Old Silk Road and substantiate Polo's narrative.

Leaving Teheran on the main southerly route to Qum, the Holy City, they turned aside at Baquilabad. As the precise position of Aveh was not marked on any of their maps, they depended entirely upon information from passers-by. Aveh, they were told, lay off the beaten track, and to reach the village they would have to cross ten or fifteen miles of raw desert. On the smooth tarmac road, Mile had been managing well on the solo bike, but now they were entering rough country, so it was decided to leave one of the machines at a caravanserai.

Riding across the sand proved to be easier than they had feared, for the searing heat had baked a stout crust on the red-brown earth, and the motorcycle could make good time, even with its double load. Tricky moments only occurred when the tyres broke through the top surface and the wheels spun themselves helplessly into the loose sand beneath the crust. But such moments were rare and there was time to reflect what a far cry it was from the traditional holly and snow of Christmas and the wondrous Magi to this salt-encrusted rolling plateau, where the horizon shimmered in advancing waves of heat. After a while, even the faintest of tracks petered out, and the two travellers began to feel the loneliness of the empty desert. Their minds were full of the tale of the Burning Well, and for want of a more reliable guide in such abandoned country they headed towards a tall column of smoke in the distance. As they journeyed, the dark pillar began to lurch towards them across the dunes, and in a moment the sky was blotted out

99

by a swirling blast of flying sand. But the dust-devil, which was their pillar of smoke, led them to Aveh. Heaving itself out of the next wadi the motorcycle topped the rise, and there, nestling below them, lay three villages, strung out in a chain around their oases.

In the central square of Aveh, the two travellers washed the brown dirt from their throats and lay down exhausted in the shade of the main well, which is the hub of life in every Persian village. A steady line of women, swathed from head to toe, pattered past with pitchers on their heads to draw water for their households. Camels swayed by; donkeys trotted along, huge nets of melons bulging at their sides, and as night came on with the sudden swiftness of the lower latitudes, the storks returned with a great flapping and bustle to their untidy nests on the roof-tops.

Inevitably, crowds began to gather in the clusters which surround any strange visitor to these isolated outposts of human survival. A little rested, Stan and Mike were taken to the house of Aveh's headman, where a meal of soup, tea and melons was hospitably provided, as they asked in halting Persian about the Three Wise Men. Not surprisingly, no one, not even the headman's son who had been to school, really understood what was meant. So the headman suggested that next morning they should ask the Wise Man of the village.

The two spent the night curled up with a few cushions on the flat roof of the box-shaped mud house. There they shared with the storks the delicious cool of the evening breeze and the magnificence of the desert night when the stars blaze so close to the earth. In such a sky had the Wise Men first seen the mystic star which led them to Bethlehem, and afterwards, the legend runs, this same constellation descended like Holy Fire, into a deep well, where it yet may be seen by the very devout.

Early next morning the headman escorted his two visitors back to the main square, where in a shady corner sat the Wise Man of the village. Too old to work, but respected for their age and knowledge, such Methusalahs are frequently found in the little villages as they squat patiently in their own little world of the past, fed and sheltered by their great-grand-children or those who have compassion for their years.

With much emphasis the headman explained the position to the old man, and although the true reason for the visit still escaped him, the old man shuffled slowly to his feet. To him, a visitor to Aveh could only have come to see one thing, for Aveh had only one curiosity to offer. They followed their guide as he hobbled, leaning on his stick, down a side lane until they were clear of the village, and reached the base of a great pentagonal mound, resembling a pyramid with its apex lopped off. Crumbling steps led to the top of the mound, and after toiling their way up, the old man stopped and pointed with his stick. Half-buried in the sand was a battered and peeling notice. Written on it, and written incredibly enough in English, were the words :—

FOR ZOROASTRIANS ONLY

The pieces of the jigsaw fell into place. Here at Aveh stood the identifiable remains of a temple, built by the Zoroastrians or Zartusti, whose religion is a thousand years older than Islam. The presence of this ancient temple was evidence that the village of Aveh had a history which stretched back to the time of Marco Polo; thus is would be reasonable to identify modern Aveh with the settlement of Polo's day, and so place it on the map of thirteenth century Persia in relation to the Old Silk Road. But this was not all. The Zoroastrian temple at Aveh was the key to one of Marco's most intriguing legends, the tale of the Fiery Well. In this story Marco Polo had described how the Three Kings after taking their leave of the Infant Christ set out for home :—

And after they had ridden for some days, they resolved to see what the child had given them (a closed casket). They opened the casket and found inside it a stone. They wondered greatly what this could be. The child had given it to them to signify that they should be as firm as stone in the faith that they had adopted. For, when the three kings had seen that the child had taken all three offerings, they concluded that he was at once a god, and an earthly king, and a healer. And, since the child knew that the three kings believed this, he gave them the stone to signify that they should be firm and constant in their belief. Then the three kings, not knowing why the stone was given to them, took it and threw it into a well. No sooner had it fallen in when there descended from heaven a burning fire, which came straight into the well into which it had been thrown. When the three kings saw this miracle, they repented of their throwing away the stone; for they saw clearly that its signific-

ance was great and good. They immediately took some of this
fire and took it to their own country and put it in one of their
churches, a noble and splendid building. They keep it perpetu-
ally burning and worship it as a god. And every sacrifice and
burnt offering they make is roasted with this fire. And if it ever
happens that this fire goes out, they go round to others who
worship fire also with the same faith and are given some of the
fire which burns in their own church. This they bring back to
rekindle their fire. They never rekindle it except with this fire
of which I have spoken. To procure this fire, they often make a
journey of ten days.

That is how it comes about that the people of this country are
fire-worshippers, and I assure you that they are very numerous.
All this was related to Messer Marco Polo by the inhabitants
of this town, and all is perfectly true.

The ruined Zoroastrian temple at Aveh was silent proof that
this story of Marco's was not a wild rumour, but based on genuine
foundations, which involved the muddling of two religions, Zoroastrianism and Christianity. The Guebers, or followers of the
prophet Zoroaster, venerated fire as the source of life and the
physical expression of the Godhead, Ahura Mazda, Lord of
Wisdom. Somehow Marco Polo must have come to hear of their
religious rites, in which the worship of fire is the supreme devotion.
From there it was but a short and logical step to transpose the
origin of the sacred Zoroastrian flames to his own Christian marvel
of the Fiery Well. Obviously this was a mistake which was very
easy to make, but it is a tribute to Polo's more customary factual
accuracy that he correctly placed the centres of fire-worship at
Saveh, Aveh and Kala Atishparastan, the last-named meaning in
Persian 'the place where they worship fire'.

In the narrow-minded gloom of the thirteenth century papacy
these extraordinary tales of fire-worship must have been no more
understandable than messages from outer space. It was lucky that
Polo could give a Christian twist to such revelations or his descriptions might have been banned by the Church as ungodly, for as
Masefield once wrote, 'in all history only five men have really
travelled and seen marvels, Ptolemy, Melchior, Caspar, Balthazar
and Marco Polo'. Unhappily, the sands of time are obscuring
many of these marvels which so shook the European world, and
Zoroastrianism itself has greatly declined in importance. Most of

the old Gueber centres were destroyed during the Arab invasion of Persia in the seventh century and the true believers subjected to severe penalties. Many Zoroastrians fled to India and there, in accordance with their religion they raised the well-known Towers of Silence, where the vultures pick the bones of the dead lest the corpses defile earth and the sacred fire. Some active traces of Zoroastrianism are still to be found in Iran and the religion has recently seen the building of several temples, one of which was endowed, curiously enough, by an English baronet. Today the town of Yezd, a day's journey from Aveh, is the main centre of the religion, and there eternal sandalwood fires still burn in the square Gueber temples, as they once did on the crest of the great worship mound at Aveh.

But Mike and Stan were not yet finished with Aveh, nor Aveh with them. For they were brought sharply back to the twentieth century when they descended from the mound and returned to the village. Standing by their motorcycle was the Chief of Aveh's Police Force. He had seen Mike filming the womenfolk washing clothes in the little stream that ran down one side of the village square. His Moslem sense of decency was outraged. He insisted that the two visitors were spies.

Now normally a few explanations would have cleared up the whole matter in a few moments, but Stan and Mike had made the grave mistake of leaving their passports behind for safe keeping at Baquilabad on the main road. 'Passport!! Passport!!', shouted the Sergeant through his moustache. There were no passports to be produced and explanations were not accepted, so the pair of spies were summarily locked up in the policeman's house, which served as the jail.

Through the key-hole of their cell door, the prisoners could see that the Police Chief was writing out a lengthy report. After much searching in various corners, the Sergeant discovered a pen which worked if he wielded it vigorously. With slow concentration he laboriously spelt out his composition. After an hour or so, when this was finished, the two captives were brought out and informed that the report would have to go to Police Branch Headquarters in a village forty miles to the west, where in due course it would be read by his superior and the sergeant would be advised what to do next.

Dismayed by all this delay and mindful of the grinding slowness of official police procedure the world over, Mike asked how long it would take for the message to reach Branch Headquarters. Not until someone going that way was able to take the note with him, was the airy reply. Quickly Stan seized his opportunity. Pointing to the motorcycle he offered to speed the process of the law by taking the report himself. The obvious plot was that Mike should leap onto the pillion seat behind as Stan drove away, and the truants would roar out of Aveh for ever. Mike, however, was at some pains to point out that not only were the constabulary heavily armed, but in all likelihood the pillion passenger would bear the brunt of a well-directed fusillade. In any case, the Sergeant had other ideas. He intended to send Stan as a courier, but only under armed escort.

Accordingly, the senior Corporal was deputized to ride behind Stan. However, the departure of the mission could hardly have been described as a crisply efficient display by the militia. Stan let in the clutch with a bang; the bike reared up like a stallion and the unfortunate Corporal flew through the air to land with a jarring crunch on the packed earth. To make matters worse, Mike, true to his profession, had somehow got hold of his camera again and succeeded in filming the farce. With a roar of rage, the Sergeant sent two of his men to frogmarch Mike back into the cell, whilst the discomforted Corporal slunk away to allow a younger and more resilient gendarme to climb on the pillion seat. This guard sacrificed all dignity in the interests of safety, and, slinging his rifle across his shoulders, clung to Stan's broad back with an anxious bear-hug. This time the motorcycle pulled docilely away, through the main gates and out into the sand hills.

Riding as pillion passenger on a battered motorcycle across the hazards of the open desert is a difficult exercise at the best of times. It is almost impossible if one has had no experience in the matter. If the driver happens to be Stan, then the task becomes super-human. For Stan is an ardent supporter of the theory that the best method of crossing rough country is to drive at top speed with the throttle jammed wide open; the idea is that the machine thereby hurtles over the top of the worst pitfalls. The simple mechanics of this progress involve extreme skidding, bumping, pitching and swaying. As the motorcycle bounds across the bumps of the ground, the heavy engine and Stan's not inconsiderable bulk pin down the front end of the vehicle. This leaves the sting in the motorcycle's tail, which whips up and down in a combined imitation of a bucking bronco and the Wall of Death. After the initial scare, the determined pillion passenger, if he has not had the good sense to get off, is thrashed into a condition of dazed stupor, like a terrier hanging on to the nose of an angry bull.

So it was with the unhappy armed guard, who was soon feeling far too battered to act coherently. In due course, as always happened, Stan lost control of the machine and in the customary spill, rolled safely clear. The gendarme was not nearly so well practised in the art, so did not display the same expertise, but lay gasping in the dust like a stranded flounder. Cautiously Stan retrieved the ancient rifle and removed the ammunition. Then he rode off by himself to fetch the passports.

In the meantime Mike had been busy in Aveh. With his genius for winning children to his cause, he rapidly organized a shuttle service of small brown hands which thrust food and cigarettes to him through the cell bars. Since the local policemen, like every other Persian, had a great affection for children, the Aveh militia were forced to relent and Mike was allowed to set up court in the little walled garden. Within a few moments he was surrounded by his wide-eyed audience of devotees, who scurried to and fro, bearing melons, grapes, tea, eggs and rice. For each offering they were rewarded with a fresh piece of comedy, and the little garden shrilled with laughter. By the time Stan returned to Aveh, Mike had almost drowned beneath a wave of popular sympathy and was sprawled contentedly on the cushions and carpet, which had been looted by the miniature conspirators from the Sergeant's own office. By then, the sole occupant of the cell was the luckless escort who had failed so miserably to look after Stan on his desert ride.

Passports were produced and examined. Stan joined the feast and a general amnesty was declared. The pact was sealed with many cups of tea and cigarettes, and then, surrounded by smiles, the two travellers left the village of the Wise Man.

Rejoining the main road at Baquilabad the second motorcycle proved a liability. The road to Isfahan deteriorated badly, and Mike, who was beginning to suffer from dysentery, was not

sufficiently experienced on a solo machine to risk the long ride to
Kabul. It was decided to send back the extra machine by train
from Qum to Teheran, and proceed two-up on one motorcycle
with Stan at the controls.

Passing through the lovely city of Isfahan with its mosques and
carpet industry, where the new carpets are soaked in the river
and left in the streets to be trampled down until they look old
enough to be priced as antique, they reached Yezd, of which
Marco Polo had said :—'Among the cities of Persia is one called
Yezd, a very fine and splendid city and a centre of commerce. A
silken fabric called Yezdi is manufactured here in quantity and
exported profitably to many markets.'

In Marco's day the commercial importance of Yezd, most
easterly city of Persia Proper, was so great that the city achieved
a golden age of self-rule under the Atabegs from the middle of the
eleventh century to the end of the thirteenth. Step by step the
land routes of the area began to wither away, and after the city
lost her independence, trade was further discouraged by the taxes,
customs, tolls and tariffs which new and rapacious rulers imposed
in an unending stream. The strangulation of Yezd's vital arteries
was a lingering decline, and even as late as 1810 a British traveller,
one Captain Christie, was able to report that the city was 'very
large and populous, situated on the edge of a sandy desert, con-
tiguous to a range of mountains running east and west. It is
celebrated by all merchants for the protection offered to specu-
lators, and the security of its inhabitants and all their property.
It is the grand mart between Hindoostan, Baghdad, Khorassan
and Persia, and it is said to be a place of greater trade than any
other in the latter Empire.' Today, Yezd is still in the front rank
of Persian cities, but has an air of decaying hopelessness as the
desert creeps ever nearer to her walls.

Where in all Yezd might Stan and Mike uncover a surviving
fragment of her renowned and ancient silk industry which Polo
had noted? In Teheran it had been easy enough to learn that
cotton, carpets and gauze are all made in present-day Yezd. On
the other hand nobody could offer any advice about the famous
Yezdi silk, twenty-five lengths of which had once formed part of
the Royal Gift from Nadir Shah to the King of Bokhara. Leaving
Mike in a tea-house to suffer out the torments of his stomach

troubles, Stan searched the old quarter of the town. Once again it was the children who were the greatest help of all. They darted here and there in shoals, pulling Stan into dark hovels wherever the mothers and sisters worked at looms. Disappointingly the products always turned out to be plain cotton goods or rather dull fuzzy carpets. Then, as he walked past a long, low line of houses with domed mud roofs, Stan heard a peculiar flapping noise coming from one of the ventilation holes. In a last attempt he knocked at the dilapidated wooden door. The noise stopped, and a youth of about sixteen appeared in the entrance. Behind him was a single room, long, low and dark. From end to end hung a great web of silken strands. Despite the deep shadow, it was possible to discern that the entire mud building was really one vast loom where the silk cloth was produced. Up one wall hung the raw threads, held taut by little bags of sand; from there the threads looped over a spacing bar, and then stretched down to the shuttle section at floor level, where, in order to operate the shuttle, the young man stood chest deep in a pit dug into the earth. The woven cloth then ran up diagonally above his head to the great spindle, revolving high up on the wall behind him. The mysterious flapping noise proved to be the sound of the lad's shirt-tail, which he attached to the shuttle so that he fanned himself as he worked.

The raw untreated silk weave was delightfully soft and delicate, the legendary fabric of the splendid East, but without the lavish decoration of its heyday, when it was famed throughout the Orient for the cunning effects of the rich needlework. Today the work of the embroiderers is far too costly to find ready markets in competition with machine-made goods. The few looms of Yezd like the one which Stan saw in the gloom of the mud shack are all that remain of an industry which was old when Marco Polo passed through Yezd at a time when many people in Europe still believed that this gossamer of luxury was woven by strange wood-dwelling Seres who worked bark, leaves and pure stream water, to produce the glorious lustre of fine silk.

From Yezd, the caravan route Marco Polo took south-east, so that

> After the traveller leaves this city (Yezd), he rides for seven
> days over a plain in which there are only three inhabited places

The Village of the Magi

where he can get shelter. Along the route there are many fine groves of date palms, which are pleasant to ride through, and abundance of wild game including partridges and quail, a great boon to merchants travelling that way ... At the end lies a kingdom called Kerman.

The Polo Caravan could not have been dawdling at this stage of the journey, for the distance from Yezd to Kerman is approximately 160 miles, and twenty-three miles per day is no mean distance for a mixed caravan. The modern road follows exactly the same line skirting the fringe of the desert of Kerman. Only nowadays the many fine groves of date palms are very few and far between. Along most of the way the gravel road is overlain with the thick dust of the parched countryside and the only vegetation is a species of low desert scrub, rattling drily in the faint gusts of hot wind. The land has been slowly dying from desiccation since the thirteenth century when Polo rode there amidst an 'abundance of wild game'. Nowadays the only living creatures are the wretched humans, huddled miserably in the straggling mud houses of the small villages. Fate has dealt hard with the unfortunate peasants. Over the ages the annual rainfall diminished and the water table sank, and inch by inch the desert has encroached inexorably on their fields and water courses.

Everywhere there are signs of the desperate struggle between man and Nature. The surface of the land lies scarred and pitted with strange lunar craters, as if the earth has been lacerated with sticks of aerial bombs. These lines of pock-marks, often stretching for miles, mark the course of underground water channels or 'quanaats', drudgingly burrowed out with bucket, scraper and windlass. 'Quanaats' are the desperate reaction of communities doomed by failing water supplies. In the distant hills the villagers tap small rock springs and grub out their subterranean tunnels to bring the precious fluid to their crops. Each pit is surrounded by a hummock where the team of human moles have thrown up the spoil of their labours. At some points the ground is riddled with an entire complex of underground galleries, running at different levels many feet below the surface. In terms of human effort the cost of each thin underground trickle is immense, for the sandy soil collapses easily, with appalling loss of life. Yet this is the price of survival and it is relevant to note that throughout Persia the

108

men from Yezd and Kerman are famous above all others for the digging of quanaats. As likely as not, the foremen of any burrowing gang carries a heavy burden of experience gained in the hardship of his own village choking in the grip of drought.

There can be little doubt that in the cycles of climatic change, the Persian peasants of Polo's day were fortunate compared with those of modern times. It is noticeable that on only one occasion does Marco mention a 'quanaat', and in that single instance he describes it uncomprehendingly as a rarity,

> A stream of fresh water which runs underground. In certain places there are caverns carved and scooped out by the action of the stream; through which it is possible to see the flowing water, then it suddenly plunges underground.

Marco Polo saw this strange water-course three full days journey north out of Kerman. Today, if one were to travel in that direction from the city, there is nothing but the sun-smashed whiteness of the Dasht-i-Lut, the Great Salt Desert. Where Polo's caravan once passed, there is now utter, awful desolation. The last camel train went north from Kerman many years ago, and only a few people are left alive who remember the caravan trail to Tabas and the regions of Khorassan.

Faced with this reality once they had reached Kerman, Stan and Mike very sensibly decided that it would be foolish to attempt to cross the terrible Dasht-i-Lut on their weary motorcycle. Moreover Mike was in considerable stomach pain, probably contracted from impure water, which, Polo warned, 'was so bitter and Brackish, that to drink one drop will cause you to void your bowels ten times over.' Instead, they arranged to call on the Director of Mines for Kerman Province in order to ask him whether he could throw any light on Polo's mention of steel manufacture in the town. The Director of Mines was helpful but unrewarding. In modern Kerman there is now no trace of the famous Kermani swordsmiths, who once upon a time could forge a blade so strong and true that it would cleave a European helm without even turning the sabre's edge.

Then, leaving Polo's route in order to keep to the modern road, Stan and Mike rode south-east to endure the scorching passage across the Baluchistan Desert, where the motorcycle had to be kept moving for fear that the petrol would vaporize in the tank. Via Quetta and the Bolan Pass, a thousand miles of heat, punctures, dust and discomfort, they reached Afghanistan and in Kabul awaited the arrival of the third member of the Marco Polo Route Project.

8

APPLES OF PARADISE

AFTER STAN AND MIKE HAD LEFT ME in Teheran, I spent a
few more days in the capital, resting my injured foot and preparing
for my journey to the Gulf of Hormuz in the extreme south of the
country. It was like organizing a completely fresh expedition. On
this occasion I would depend entirely upon local transport, for my
range of movement was severely limited on the crude wooden
crutches which were fixed up for me in the bazaar. Having bought
a rucksack, I filled it with a sleeping bag, spare sweater, fresh
socks and my precious copy of Polo's Journal. I also acquired a
stout water bottle and fierce-looking sheath knife, tucking the
latter neatly and unobtrusively in the top of my left boot. The
other boot I hopefully stowed in the bottom of the rucksack against
the day when I would remove the Plaster of Paris and use my
damaged foot once more.

Thus prepared, I limped down to the main bus terminus in
Teheran, and climbed aboard the coach to Isfahan. Over the next
two months I was destined to spend a great deal of time in every
kind and class of bus, ranging from big Mercedes coaches to
broken-down converted lorries. Transport in Persia and Afghanistan is dominated by buses, because there are few railways or
private cars outside the main cities. There are American buses,
German buses, British buses and Russian buses. Each brand has
its own price and reputation. To travel from Teheran to Isfahan
in an American coach costs about 18/-, though the same journey

by converted lorry can be accomplished for as little as 3/-. The big bus companies with large fleets levy a fixed charge, but small local concerns, with perhaps only one vehicle, fix their price according to circumstances. If you look poor and there are only a few other passengers that day, the fare is cheap; if trade is brisk and you exude prosperity, then your fare may well be doubled or tripled. The scene at a bus terminal is reminiscent of a nineteenth century coaching stop. Drivers saunter past with a casually professional air, while their handymen cry out the merits of their particular vehicle. Urchins importune for baksheesh, as solid-looking porters strip you of your baggage and heave it on board. The bewildered passenger is battered, jostled and barged in a forest of outstretched hands and a cacophony of shouts, which rises to a frantic crescendo as each bus lurches on its way.

Most drivers prefer to set off at five in the morning to cover as much ground as possible before the main heat of the day. But before the bus starts, the fares must be collected from impecunious customers, cases strapped on the roof rack, and seating finalized. Sheep, children, chickens, and goats are passed from hand to hand down the central gangway which serves as an additional aisle of seats. Passengers pay more for sitting in the front of the bus, less for the rear, and least of all if they are content to huddle in the gangway. The craftiest customers manage to hitch-hike a couple of miles out of town beyond the police limits and then flag down the bus at the roadside. In this case, they pay the driver two or three shillings for their illicit ride to the outskirts of the next main town, when they hop off a short distance before the usual police control post. The driver does well out of this system, for he pockets the money from his 'ghost' passengers.

The drivers themselves are well respected. They must hold a special driving licence, Driving Licence Number One, which is only given after a stiff police examination, both theoretical and practical, including vehicle maintenance. This is not surprising when one considers that a bus-driver in the wild area is more like the Captain of a ship. His word is law, and his skill may mean the difference between life and death if his vehicle is stranded half-way across the desert. The job is well paid and he can earn as much as £3-£4 per day, plus a percentage of the money his passengers spend at the wayside roadhouses. The bus companies pay the drivers acording to skill and experience, but also for the route they cover. Coaxing an old decrepit vehicle on gravel paths across the desert is better paid than driving a new diesel coach on tarmac roads. Each driver picks his own assistant and a grease boy to ride with him and guard the bus, for it is nothing unusual to be on the move for eighteen hours in the day and the strain is immense. Punctures, break-downs, bandits, floods, sandstorms and quarelling passengers require that every bus driver is mechanic, diplomat and psychiatrist rolled into one.

Being a passenger on such a bus is a unique experience. To begin with, the bus company cunningly unscrews the seats from their original positions and concertinas each row, so that two more tiers of seats can then be added. It is not that the local passengers are of smaller stature, but more fares can be packed in on each haul, so there is more profit to be had. Under these conditions a broken foot encased in plaster bears some resemblance to a ball and chain. One is wedged immovably into position, knees pressing against the seat in front and the small of one's back jammed into the rear support. Any wriggle forces your next-door neighbour to shift his position as well, and he usually ends up by treading heavily on your bare toes nakedly vulnerable beyond the rigid limits of the plaster. This goes on unendingly as the bus rattles its way at a steady 35 m.p.h. over the interminable countryside. At two-hourly intervals there is a tea-stop. The bus wheezes to a halt by a caravanserai and everyone climbs out for refreshment. Afterwards, before the journey resumes, every living creature must be shoe-horned back into place, often with considerable strife over seating space established by precedent. Occasionally one bus manages to catch up with another vehicle from a rival firm operating along the same route. Then like a knight of old the adversary must yield the passage, and your driver fiercely speeds along for mile after mile close behind his opponent. With one hand on the raucous horn demanding to be let by, your champion seems totally oblivious to the fog of dust which pours in at every window, blinding and choking the passengers. On a different occasion, the other driver turns out to be a friend, and the contents of the two buses swelter whilst their drivers embrace like long-lost brothers, even though they saw each other at the terminus that same morning.

Travelling by bus does have some compensations. It may be dusty and very, very uncomfortable. One may see only a small part of the countryside through the dirty windows, but bus travel is comparatively cheap and one does meet people. Indeed, no one can escape, yourself included. Everyone is united by discomfort and the excitement of the journey. A solitary European is the natural focus of curiosity and a steady flow of sweetmeats, dried watermelon seeds and other titbits which look highly dubious when presented twentieth-hand. Nevertheless, one must swallow the offering, for hurt feelings are more important than an upset stomach, and it does relieve the monotony.

Without a doubt, monotony is the chief enemy. It took two days to travel from Teheran to Kerman by bus, and the scenery never appeared to change. When we left Teheran, the bus to all appearances was packed to repletion, but all the same the driver was constantly stopping to pick up additional wayfarers. All the way from Teheran to Isfahan my plaster foot bounced merrily on the vibrating steel floor as the bus rattled furiously along, and my only consolation was the thought that the second phase from Isfahan to Kerman would be even less comfortable if that were conceivable. I was not mistaken. During the second day the temperature rose and the road went from bad to worse. We had five punctures before landfall at Kerman after midnight, and, too exhausted to move, I slept till dawn high on the roof-rack, crutches and all.

My visit to Kerman was connected with the fact that 689 years earlier, the three Polos too had reached the city. There they arranged to join a caravan wending south to the ancient port of Hormuz, which lies on the Gulf of Hormuz over against the Trucial Oman States. The Polos' plan was to embark at Hormuz on one of the dhows, which, by making use of the monsoon winds, slant across the Arabian Sea to India. After that, the Venetians would have been able to cross to Malaysia, and then travel to Peking on board one of the Chinese trading fleets which regularly visited South-east Asia. But when they reached Hormuz the three travellers discovered that the vessels in the port were 'very bad and many of them founder ... which makes it a risky undertaking to sail in these ships.' Perhaps the Polos, as Venetians with their high standards of shipbuilding, were being over-critical, but the fact

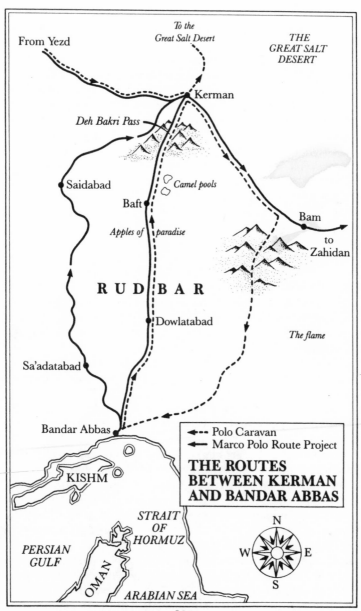

From Yezd

To the
Great Salt Desert

THE
GREAT SALT
DESERT

Kerman

Deh Bakri Pass

Saidabad

Camel pools

Baft

Bam

Apples of paradise

to
Zahidan

R U D B A R

Dowlatabad

The flame

Sa'adatabad

Bandar Abbas

← - - Polo Caravan
←— Marco Polo Route Project

**THE ROUTES
BETWEEN KERMAN
AND BANDAR ABBAS**

KISHM

*STRAIT
OF
HORMUZ*

N

*PERSIAN
GULF*

W   E

OMAN

S

ARABIAN SEA

115

remains that they preferred the unknown dangers of the overland trail to the known hazards of the ocean voyage, so the caravan turned back to Kerman by a different route to the one it had taken to reach Hormuz and began the fantastic trans-continental route through Persia, Afghanistan and the Gobi Desert to Cathay.

My intention was to discover exactly which two trails Marco Polo had used on his way through the mountains to Hormuz and then back to Kerman. There were three known tracks through the mountains, one of which had never been examined in the light of Marco Polo's narrative of this route. Colonel Yule, the greatest Polian authority, had written that 'until the direct route through Baft has been travelled, we cannot be sure of the precise route to Hormuz'. I intended not only to travel this particular trail for myself, but also find out all that was possible about the other tracks through the mountains, and then compare them with Marco's account. This, in theory, would prove rewarding, for Marco's description of the journey from Kerman to Hormuz is amongst the most carefully detailed sections of his book. He is at pains to emphasize that their caravan took two different roads; one to reach Hormuz, and another path for the return trip after the decision not to set sail from the port. On the outward journey Marco notes a seven days' ride across a pleasant plateau; a mountain pass which is intensely cold in winter; and a broad fertile plain rich in wheat, dates, pistachios and berries, where the traveller encounters magnificent hawks, turtle-doves and francolins. There also he saw humped cattle and fat-tailed sheep. But, Marco warns, the traveller must beware because the path is infested with 'villainous bands of cut-throat robbers'.

The account of Marco Polo's journey at this stage is sufficiently detailed to allow his exact track to be plotted from village to village. However, the problem is not entirely straight forward, because some of his references are extremely puzzling; for example Marco writes that he found the 'apples of Paradise'. Most important, the country between Hormuz and Kerman is some of the worst in Persia. It is the land of the Sard or 'Cold' Mountains and the Rudbar, the 'plateau of streams'. In places the mountains rise to 14,500 feet, about the height of the Matterhorn, elsewhere there is a jumbled rocky plateau. The region is virtually uninhabited and forms a neglected corner of modern Iran. Despite this, my

Above: Departure from north Oxford

Right: Yugoslavia: great interest in British motorcycles

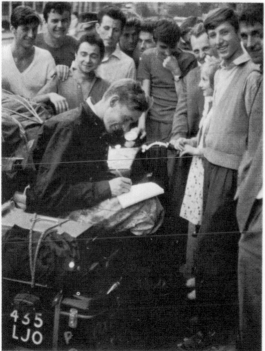

Above: Negotiating for
motorbike repairs in
Belgrade

Right: Mike

Facing page:

Above: Istanbul: mealtime
with Arghun's family

Below: Goreme: the village
headman

Above: Erzinjan: an 'ehram' loom

Right: An 'ehram' swathed figure

Facing page:

Above: Stan and Tim in Polo's 'finest baths anywhere to be found'

Below: Turkey: about to jettison the sidecar

Left: Biluchi camelman

Below: 'The vessels built at Hornuz are dangerous for navigation' – Marco Polo

Facing page:

Above: Skin and wattle caravanserai of the Apples of Paradise

Below: Persia: preparing a caravanserai meal

Left: Aveh: the wise man of
the village

Below: Three on one
motorcyle

personal mission was to traverse it in both directions, just as Polo had once done.

The obvious place to start my investigations was the bazaar in Kerman. So I stumped my way between the stalls, enquiring if anyone could tell me about the country to the south. Everyone advised me to ask Old Rezakhan, the great landlord of the Rudbar, who had held much land to the south. I found him at his stately home on the outskirts of the town. Courtly and old-fashioned from a less hurried generation, he entertained me in his delightful walled garden where the doves fluttered in the cool trees. Over glasses of sweet tea we talked in English of the great caravan days of his youth. He remembered clearly his own journey to Hormuz over the Sarvizan Pass with a large train of 200 mules, camels and horses, ladened with grapes, pistachios, almonds, carpets and cotton goods. It had been almost the last great caravan to the coast, and from his diary he read out the record of the journey. The tale I heard was so like Polo's description that I knew that the first leg of Marco's route was no longer in doubt. Old Reza-khan described how the way through the Sarvizan led to a cold mountain pass and the fertile plateau of Marco's account. He even mentioned the turtle-doves, hawks and francolins. To cap it all, both caravan journeys, though separated by over 600 years, had taken seventeen days. Old Rezakhan had known the mountains since childhood, and he had no hesitation in explaining that only one mountain track matched Marco Polo's description. To-gether we traced on my map the trail which the Venetian caravan must have taken southward.

However, all this information merely corroborated a journey which had been carried out by a Major R. M. Smith, R.E. in 1866. For many years it had been accepted that Polo went South by the Sarvizan. So far I had only confirmed what was already known. It was left for me to investigate Marco's return journey back to Kerman from Hormuz. Here Rezakhan could only advise me that there were two possible routes. The first skirted around the Western flank of the Sard Mountains via Saida-bad. This was also the modern motor road. The alternative and more attractive trail led high over the Deh Bakri Pass via Baft through the heart of the upland. It seemed to me that the obvious course of action was to follow both routes and see which one coincided most closely with Polo's description of his own path. Old Rezakhan was horrified. He pointed out that, although the motor road was perfectly safe, he would not be held responsible if I travelled in the mountains. None of the townsfolk ventured into the hills, for they harboured wild nomad tribesmen who were a law unto themselves, criminals and outlaws. A few months earlier a police patrol looking for wanted fugitives had been ambushed and wiped out. Even Rezakhan's own tenant farmers in the foothills had to be allotted rifles for their defence. Besides, the only people who used the Deh Bakri Pass nowadays were shady characters who wished to avoid the police control posts on the lowland motor route.

But by now I was determined to do justice to Polo, whose writing had so often been maligned for lack of accuracy. If it were humanly possible, I would cross the Deh Bakri Pass in the hope of proving once again the remarkable precision of Marco's tale. Gratefully thanking old Rezakhan, I returned to the bazaar and haggled a ride on a very ancient and dishevelled truck that was due to leave in the general direction of the Deh Bakri. Scrambling up on top of the cargo of rock sugar in the company of eighteen Persian peasants, a dozen chickens, and a couple of horned sheep, we clattered out over the rough tracks across the bleak plain. My plaster foot was the object of much curious prodding accompanied by expressions of wonder, eventually making a very convenient seat for a small boy. The never-failing medium of my cracked, tuneless singing eroded away the initial reserve of my travelling companions, and soon we were rolling merrily along to a broken version of the Eton Boating Song, accompanied by the flapping of long shirt-tails in the slipstream, as my colleagues clung on to the bouncing lorry with one hand and their black Derby hats with the other. There was no doubt in their minds that I was mad, a soul afflicted of Allah, and they gleefully spread the news at every roadside hamlet.

I was the only remaining passenger when the lorry wheezed to a halt at its journey's end, the last of the foothill settlements. As the sun rose next morning, I hobbled happily around the village on my crutches, photographing a miniature Venetian scene, where the mud houses lined pleasant water courses and wandering minstrels plucked their lutes to audiences of peasants squatting in the shade. Unfortunately the sight of a camera once again brought trouble. I was hauled off to jail by the local police. A soldier, complete with rifle, was posted on each side of the door, but when it was obvious that I had no intention of making a one-legged escape, both my sentries very wisely fell fast asleep. After his lunch, the Sergeant in Command summoned me for interrogation. Did I have a permit to leave Kerman? he asked. No, I had never even heard of such a document, and my passport, visas and other papers entirely failed to impress him. Then, as luck would have it, I unearthed from the bottom of my rucksack the embossed sheet of paper which testified to my fully paid-up Associate Membership of the Royal Geographical Society. For a document which was really no more than a receipt for my annual subscription, the membership certificate worked wonders. The Sergeant took it reverently from my hand, and holding it upside down so that the crest became a seal, he scanned it with considerable respect. Then he peeled off a crisp salute and shot out a string of rapid-fire commands. Policeman A was ordered to carry my rucksack, and Policeman B was to instruct his wife to prepare a meal for me.

Later, through the efforts of my blue-uniformed accomplices, I found myself ensconced in the passenger seat of yet another lorry, this time heading farther into the barren hills towards my objective, the Deh Bakri Pass. Steadily we progressed, often in reverse gear, having to grind backwards up the sides of the wadis, which served as motor tracks. Then, without warning, the driver over-reached himself and the truck toppled majestically down a steep bank. Crawling out into the dust amidst the trickles of oil, petrol and water, my first reaction was to check whether I had succeeded in smashing any more bones. Luckily the spill had been relatively gentle, and neither the driver, the lorry nor I were damaged. Stoically the driver trudged off back the way we had come. Equally resigned, I settled down in the shade of the up-turned vehicle to await the appearance of enough villagers to heave the lorry back onto its well-worn tyres.

While I was contemplating the dull middle distance, there appeared the totally unexpected figure of a Baluchi tribesman riding a camel along the rim of the wadi. I do not know who was the more surprised—the Baluchi in his baggy robes and untidy turban, or the crippled Englishman sitting mildly in the middle of nowhere. Nevertheless, it was obviously much too good an opportunity to be missed. Within a moment I was perched up on the beast's hump with my crutches tucked firmly under the girth, while the camelman walked ahead with the leading rope.

Towards sunset we came up with some more Baluchi and a group of about twenty camels clustered in a secluded rendezvous. After much bartering in broken Persian and sign language amidst the bubbling, groaning beasts, I paid my passage with them through the Deh Bakri Pass. Tactfully, I was content to accept my phenomenal luck in finding a way of travelling the Pass, and refrained from asking what sort of business took the Baluchi by such abandoned trails. Ostensibly the camels were slung with sacks of grain, but bearing in mind Old Rezakhan's warning, I concluded that the Baluchi were making a lucrative sideline of smuggling, probably taking hashish from the Quayen area of Khorassan down to the dhows at Bandar Abbas.

At nightfall the temperature plummetted after the heat of the day, or as Marco had put it, the cold is 'so intense that it can scarcely be warded off by any number of garments and furs,' and under such conditions my sleeping bag was very welcome, causing a sensation with the tribesmen. When the sun warmed us next morning the camels were prodded to their feet and our little band set out at the slow, steady pace of the Baluchi camelmen. Swaying along on the hump, with my broken foot sticking out awkwardly to one side, was a thoroughly unnerving experience, especially when the camel buckled itself into the kneeling position. The lurching see-saw made me feel sure that at any moment I would tumble off ingloriously, so I clung on grimly even when the caravan stopped to let the camels graze on the scrub, whilst their owners sat down in a close huddle, gnawing coarse flat bread and cheese. The latter was gouged out of a crude bag made from an uncured kid's skin, which, although it looked and smelt revolting kept the cheese moist and soft in the blazing heat.

The novelty of travelling by camel soon wore off. The Baluchi were in no hurry and the scabby beasts proceeded at a soft-footed slouch in their own peculiarly supercilious manner. The movement of their necks reminded me strongly of a snake raising itself off the ground, and when viewed all day from behind, the ungainly hindquarters of the next camel in line with its rat-like tail, had very little to recommend it. From my observations I found no cause to envy Marco his three and a half years of similar wandering.

During the day our climb was concealed within the length of a winding ravine, which brought us out on the saddle of the Deh Bakri. Across the divide of the Pass, the trail sloped down in a series of step-like valley basins, each linked by narrow sandstone gorges. The basin floors were dry, flat sheets of small rocks and stones, left by flash floods after the tremendous thunderstorms which bring the only rainfall of the year. It was a bleak harsh country where human settlement is pitifully sparse, and the only living souls were stray groups of nomad tribesmen drifting along with their camels, as they trekked north on their annual migration to the summer encampment.

That second night our little caravan halted on the floor of one of the rock basins. Our evening meal consisted of two chickens which had spent the day flapping unhappily, hanging upside down from a saddle strap. As dusk fell the men lounged around, passing a solitary cigarette from hand to hand. The flames from the brushwood fire flickered gaunt shadows across their hawk-like faces, and beyond the ring of light the humped shapes of the resting camels merged with the thorn bushes. Ali, the self-appointed leader of the band, came over to where I sat with my damaged leg propped out uncomfortably in front of me.

'The price of your passage was not sufficient,' he said, and my heart sank with memories of the trouble in the Assassin Valley.

'We agreed the price and made a bargain,' was my reply.

'But you must pay more money now, for I did not include the price of your food, and we must buy more chickens,' stated Ali flatly.

'How much do you need?' I asked.

'Three hundred tuman.'

'But I do not have so much money with me,' I expostulated.

'Three hundred tuman,' repeated Ali, 'or we will leave you here by yourself when we move on in the morning.'

Numbly I realized what the threat implied. Left alone, miles from water with my useless foot, it was quite likely that I would die of thirst before a wandering nomad came across our bivouac. I should have heeded Polo's words that 'among the people of these kingdoms there are many who are brutal and bloodthirsty ... unless the merchants are well armed and equipped with bows, they slay and harry them unmercifully.' Making up my mind, I called Ali closer. As he squatted down beside me, I lashed out and seized his jerkin so that he was wrenched forward off balance. At the same time I pulled out the heavy knife which had remained hidden in my boot and thrust the point beneath his chin. It was a vain gesture, for I was crippled and outnumbered. In fact I had only the haziest notion of how to finish the job, and my hand was quivering with fright. Perhaps Ali mistook this for anger, because the display of violence had the desired effect. Partly from surprise but more probably from an inverted respect for my bravado, Ali gave in. Relaxing, he apologized and then scrambled free.

The only thing for me to do was to wait until the situation blew over. If the smugglers had so wished, it would have been ridiculously easy to dispose of me. I did not sleep that night in a feeble attempt to keep up my guard. But I need not have worried. The Baluchi must have decided that I was mad, utterly and completely touched in the head, and they were content to leave me in peace. As we resumed march, their attitude softened, and Ali himself became solicitous in attending to my needs, bringing the waterskin and helping me into the saddle. All the same, I decided to leave the Baluchi as soon as possible.

My opportunity came when we entered the first real village since the Pass. By then, the Baluchi had grown more accustomed to my presence and our relationship was really quite friendly. Before we parted company, I promised, to their evident relief, that I would tell no one of their presence in the area, and with that, I settled down in the village to await a less hazardous mode of transport.

To arrive at a definite association between the Baluchi trail and Marco Polo's route, I needed more evidence. As I waited, my thoughts were full with conjectures about Marco's description of his path, which had led 'where mineral springs abound, good for ailments of the skin. And the bread is so bitter that no one can eat of it unless accustomed to it. This is due to the bitterness of the water.' Ali had told me that there were small sulphur pools in the nearby hills, where the nomads sometimes washed their camels to cure the worst sores, but to be fully satisfied I needed definite corroboration. As I sat down to the inevitable supper of māst (yoghourt) and nān (bread), my first mouthful confirmed that I was indeed following in Polo's footsteps. The rough flat loaf of bread was so acrid to the taste that I found it almost impossible to swallow, let alone chew. The astringent impact of each morsel contracted the throat with the bitterness of quinine, its sharp lingering taste was difficult to rinse from one's palate. No wonder Polo had remembered the unpalatable bread of the high plateau 'so bitter that no one can eat it unless he is accustomed to it'. Even this had not changed over the centuries that separated Marco Polo's visit from my own. Much later, I discussed the phenomenon of the bitter bread with the Director of Agricultural Research in Southern Persia. From the expert I learnt that the bitterness came not from the water, as Marco surmised, but from small black grains of diseased wheat included in the harvest. Furthermore, in the entire country there was only one tiny district where this particular disease was to be found. The unique instance of the bitter bread was evidence that caravans, both ancient and modern, followed trails which are decided by natural features and maintained by necessity or tradition.

In due course there turned up in the village of the bitter bread a small truck which was on its way with a load of water-melons to a chrome mine nearer the coast. I hitched a ride and rode with it through a continuing series of valley basins, each larger and more fertile than the one before. The countryside grew noticeably more prosperous, or in Marco's words, 'fine trees and date-palms abound, and the place is amply stocked with foodstuffs'. In front of our wheels, flocks of small black partridge scuttled peep-peeping into the shelter of the shrub on the verge. Once we met a tribesman walking down the dusty track, dangling a caged hawk from one hand. I would dearly have liked to witness Polo's assertion that these falcons 'fly at such incalculable speed that there is no bird which can escape from them by flight'.

A few miles from the chrome mine, the truck pulled up by the most desolate of all caravanserais, a crude aboriginal shelter of camelthorn draped with rotting skins. As the driver and I waited inside the tepee for the woman of the house to prepare our meal, the landlord crawled in, and with an air of pride held out in his gnarled hand a small, wizened fruit, much like a crab apple. With considerable mental reservations I accepted the gift, only to be encouraged with vehement gestures to eat it as a delicacy. Fearing the worst, I nibbled a tiny flake. To my surprise the fruit was delicious. It tasted like a subtle blend of plum and apple, enhanced with a touch of peach-like fragrance. Greedily I devoured the remainder of the fruit, before it dawned on me that I had stumbled across the solution to a Polian puzzle, the mysterious Apples of Paradise. None of the learned authorities on Polo's Journal had been able to decide exactly what Marco meant when he said that the fruits of the road included 'Apples of Paradise'. Some scholars had suggested that he was describing plantains, or even pineapples. But, having savoured one for myself, I appreciated without any hesitation why Marco had given the apt name 'the Apple of Paradise' to the type of nectarine which the Persians call 'shelail'.

A few miles farther on, the lorry reached the chrome mine, which was run by an English manager, who, after his initial surprise at my unexpected arrival from across the mountains, was extremely hospitable. So much so, that I was reluctant to leave for the last stage by ore truck to Bandar Abbas, the modern equivalent of Hormuz. By then, I was satisfied that my own route was identical with the track of the Venetian caravan, and I had come to trust Marco's word implicitly, relaxing in the enjoyable expectation of encountering more living examples of his medieval description.

As the Gulf Coast approached, the temperature soared. Across low ground the familiar white saltpans stretched to the horizon, broken only by the wavering spouts of small dust-devils. On the hillsides, parties of nomads moved in scattered specks against the green and white mottling of the serpentine rocks. Because of the heat, the local caravanserais were simple wicker shelters, built on platforms of boughs laid across the streamlets, so that the cool breeze could filter in refreshingly on every side, for 'in summer they would all die of the heat . . . so they build arbours of hurdles, resting at one end on the bank and at the other on piles driven below water, and covered with foliage to fend off the sun.'

The littoral was very noticeably a meeting ground unequalled in Persia. Slavers, traders and settlers sailing north from Africa had left their mark on the people of the coastal plain. In some of the hamlets, the dark skin and almost negroid features of the peasants betrayed African blood, which had led Marco Polo to comment that 'the people here are black and worship Mahomet'. An Arab influence, too, was represented by the occasional burnous and Saluki hound, and the Indian way of life had made its mark in villages where Zebu cattle stood patiently under wooden load-carrying saddles, held by straps round their humps, tails and bellies. Of these cattle Marco had written :

> The beasts also are different. Let me tell you first about the oxen. They are of great size and pure white like snow. Their hair is short and smooth because of the heat. Their horns are thick and stumpy, not pointed. Between their shoulders they have a round hump fully two palms in height. They are the loveliest things in the world to look at. When you want to load them, they lie down like camels; then, when they are loaded, they stand up and carry their loads very well because they are exceedingly strong.

Throughout history the little harbour on the shores of the Gulf of Hormuz has dominated the coastal plain. From here culture, government and trade have radiated out into the villages of the interior. The port is the hub, kernel and nucleus of its hinterland, where all roads lead ultimately to the quayside. Naturally the ore truck on which I was riding, was also heading for the wharf, and in due course we came in sight of the diminutive port of Bandar Abbas. Here on the fringe of the tropical blue waters, lapping the low sweep of coastline, I clambered down and stumped off to investigate the modern descendant of Marco's 'fine city called Hormuz'.

9

HORMUZ TO HERAT

After two days' ride he (the traveller) reaches the Ocean. Here on the coast stands a city called Hormuz, which has an excellent harbour. Merchants come here by ship from India, bringing all sorts of spices and precious stones and pearls and cloths of silk, gold and elephants' teeth and many other wares. In this city they sell them to others, who distribute them to various customers throughout the length and breadth of the world. It is a great centre of commerce, with many cities and towns subordinate to it, and the capital of the kingdom. Its king is named Ruemedan Ahmed. The climate is torrid, owing to the heat of the sun, and unhealthy. If a merchant dies here, the king confiscates all his possessions. . . . The natives do not eat our sort of food, because a diet of wheat bread and meat would make them ill. To keep them well they eat dates and salt fish, that is, tunny, and also onions; and on this diet they thrive. . . . In this district they sow their wheat and barley and other grains in November, and have got in all their harvest before the end of March. And so with all their fruits : by March they are ripened and done with. After that you will find no vegetation anywhere except date-palms, which last till May. This is due to the great heat which withers them up. . . . In summer they do not stay in the cities, or they would all die of the heat.

IT WAS NOT DIFFICULT to appreciate why Marco Polo's description of Hormuz should be dominated by his account of the terrific heat. In mid-summer the more wealthy residents still on occasion take ship to withdraw to Kuwait or Bahrein, which, they affirm, are refreshingly cool at that season, compared to their own city. Hobbling through the city a little after dawn on an August morning, it was already so hot that runnels of sweat ran down the length of my wooden crutches leaving a trail of damp patches in the dust of the street. Earlier that same morning, the water from the storage tank on the bus-station roof had been warm enough, as it spouted from the tap, to provide a comfortable shave.

In recent decades the population of Bandar Abbas has been steadily dwindling, for the port had sadly declined in importance since Marco's day. At that time the city formed a natural transhipping point on the Old Silk Road. At Hormuz, caravans from the interior linked up with dhows fanning out on their trading passages as far afield as Java and Zanzibar. It is obvious from the description in Polo's Journal that Hormuz was poised lucratively at a vital joint in the trading chain, and through the harbour flowed much of the riches of the known world. Nearly all major trading nations maintained their local agents in the shadow of the King's Palace, and the commercial status of the city rivalled that of Constantinople, which in many ways it resembled.

The actual site of the city of Hormuz oscillated from the shore-line, where Nearchus beached Alexander the Macedon's ships nearly a thousand years before the Polo visit, to a better defensive position on a rocky offshore island, a move normally brought about by the increasing audacity of brigands descending from the hills. At all times the city's prosperity varied directly with the politics of Persia, and in particular of the Kingdom of Kerman, whose natural outlet the port formed. At the beginning of the sixteenth century the city seemed to have become firmly established on the island when it was captured in 1507 for the Portuguese by Alfonso Alberqueque. But following the fierce mercantile rivalry with other European nations and the improvements in monsoon navigation across the Indian Ocean, Hormuz slumped from a vantage point to an appendix, by-passed by the more direct oceanic route between the Cape of Good Hope and the Orient. Thereafter the main value of Hormuz was as a gateway for the introduction of the Indies trade to the Persian hinterland. In 1622 the death blow was delivered by an expedition under Shah Abbas, aided by a British squadron despatched in the interests of the East

India Company. Hormuz Island was captured and the Portuguese garrison expelled. All fortifications and public buildings were razed, and the port transplanted back to the mainland village of Gambrun, which was re-named Bandar (Port) Abbas. But the Great Age of Discovery was at its peak, changing the entire focal pattern of trade, and the new port never really survived the shock of removal. Bandar Abbas slowly sank into the backwater which it is today.

At present, the 'chief seat of opulence, splendour and luxury in the Eastern world', as it was once described in an early Historical Disquisition, is a sleepy provincial town dreaming of vast improvement schemes, but at the moment entirely dependent upon a single wooden jetty, built to supply a British Expeditionary Force. Nevertheless, Bandar Abbas has a special and a very real charm of its own, despite the heat and stagnation. Life continues at a torpid pace in the merchants' houses, though nearly all trade is carried in a few wooden coasting vessels and the big steamers only call very rarely.

In the narrow alleys around the jetty there is a strongly Arab atmosphere. Between the boats and the warehouses file lines of half-naked porters, their bodies streaming with sweat as they hump their loads to a rhythmic, stamping chant of 'Yek, doh, seh, —Ya Allah!'.* On each side of the pier lie three or four wooden vessels of up to 200 tons each. Broad beamed and heavy, they rise and fall lethargically in the sleek swell of the warm salt water, their huge rudders creaking softly in the chocks. Each boat carries a short stubby mast and a stout boom to take advantage of a sailing breeze, but they depend upon old, well-tried diesel engines to chug between coastal havens. The mixed cargoes are stowed in a single central hold, and the stern of each boat rises to a blunt square poop. There, under a bleached awning, hang the provisions for the voyage, dark-brown bunches of dates, sides of raw meat and damp earthenware pitchers of water. The coasters exude an air of sturdy workmanlike efficiency in contrast to the slim shapes of small lateen-rigged dhows slipping slenderly through the water, their sides and sterns decorated with striking blue and white painted whorls.

*'One, two, three—Oh Allah!'

How much the shape of the coasters owes to European ship design is difficult to say, but in many ways they resemble the coastal craft of the Kutch. At any rate, they can be little different from the boats which Marco saw;—'Their ships,' he says, 'are very bad, and many of them founder because they are not fastened with iron nails but are stitched together with thread made of coconut husks. They soak the husk until it assumes the appearance of horsehair; then they make it into threads and stitch their ships. It is not spoilt by the salt water, but lasts remarkably well. The ships have one mast, one rudder and are not decked; when they have loaded them, they cover the cargo with hides and on top of these they load the horses that are taken to India for sale. They have not iron for nails, so they employ wooden pegs and stitch with thread. Another feature of these ships is that they are not caulked with pitch, but anointed with a sort of fish-oil.'

Judged by comparison with European maritime achievements, Marco's criticism of the Hormuz shipping is unnecessarily harsh. The coastwise traffic in the Gulf was, even in his age, seaworthy, well established and fairly reliable. Certainly, the Arab sailors were as accomplished navigators as any in Europe at that time. More probably Marco Polo's censure was directed at the actual details of the ship construction, which could scarcely compare with the painstaking excellence of the renowned ship-yards at Venice's Arsenal, where oaken keel-pieces were seasoned under water for twelve years before being fashioned into the backbone of a war galley.

The methods and means of shipbuilding as Marco saw it on the shores of the Straits of Hormuz still exist virtually unchanged. Indeed, there is little need for change when the materials and functions of small coasters in the region have not altered over the centuries. Two or three miles along the beach from Bandar Abbas is a small colony of shipwrights. A collection of half-a-dozen families, they have existed there undisturbed, with their entire lives devoted to the construction of boats in the manner Marco described. From raw timber they laboriously fashion the skeleton of the vessel with axe, saw, adze and fire. A line of men squatting in the shade of a strip of sailcloth, carefully shape the long timber lying between them. Each builder works on his own section of the beam, burning, gouging, chipping, drilling and scraping. Yet where the sections join, there is a perfect unity between the work of each man. Coconut husk is no longer used for stitching planks together, nor fish oil for waterproofing, but coir is masticated into crude oakum caulking. Iron nails are still scarce and expensive, so in their place wooden trenails are used to pin together the main joinery, a system unchanged since the thirteenth century craftsmen. Bit by bit the vessel is put together, until it begins to tower gauntly over its dwarf-like makers. In the shade of their creation the families of ship-wrights work and live in the manner of Noah and his household. Their flimsy homes are thrown up like swallows' nests against the lee of the boat's bulk, until the vessel is ready to be dragged down the beach to the water's edge on hardwood rollers, and set a-voyaging. The men who fashioned her remain, exposed upon the sweep of dazzling sand until they throw up yet another skeleton which will be the crux of their existence for the next two or three years.

After visiting the colony of shipbuilders, I returned to the merchant quarter in Bandar Abbas to find out more about Polo's description of the port. Like everyone else seeking information in the town, I gravitated to the warehouse cum office emporium of Mr. Biluchi, chief merchant of Bandar Abbas. The old man himself, in a braided skull cap, sat at the place of honour behind an antique desk decorated with ageing dusty ledgers. In dim recesses and corners rose mysterious mounds of bulging sacks and neatly rolled bales of cloth. The air cloyed heavily with the pungence of a hundred different spices lying in the warehouse, and the sticky smells of the street fruit-stalls wafted in through the ever-open door. On all sides sat or lounged Persians, Kuwaitis, Arabs and Indians, sipping Çay and smoking cigarette after cigarette. For the favoured few, a grizzled retainer tottered in with a hookah pipe, and the mouthpiece was passed appreciatively from hand to hand in solemn ritual. The talk was of commodity prices and ships' lading; exchange rates and bills of sale; loans, cinnamon, sugar, wood, pepper and mustard. Now and then Mr. Biluchi would jot down a note in his ledger and a merchant slipped out to arrange the practical organization of a deal he had just made; another trader was always ready to take his place. Each man brought with him a servant or an apprentice, and these stood patiently along the outside wall, ready to run for a ledger, a fly whisk or a box of matches. In the leisurely pace of mercantile life, marked by the replenishing of Çay glasses, there was all the time in the world to spend discussing the merits of a particular sea-captain or the price of five sacks of pistachios. At Bandar Abbas the merchants conducted business in the unhurried fashion of their forefathers.

When I arrived at the gathering, a chair was found for me and Mr. Biluchi himself answered my questions, for my presence provided a welcome diversion.

Nobody at the assembly had heard of Marco Polo but they all listened with polite attention as I read out his description of medieval Hormuz. In particular I asked for information about Marco's tale of the Burning Wind in which he said :—

> ... It is a fact that several times in the summer there comes a wind from the direction of the sandy wastes that lie around this plain, a wind so overpoweringly hot that it would be deadly if it did not happen that, as soon as men are aware of its approach, they plunge neck-deep into the water and so escape from the heat. To show just how hot this wind can be, Messer Marco gives the following account of something that happened when he was in these parts. The King of Kerman, not having received the tribute that was due to him from the Lord of Hormuz, resolved to seize this opportunity when the men of Hormuz were living outside the city in the open. He accordingly mustered 1,600 horses and 5,000 foot soldiers and sent them across the plain of Rudbar to make a surprise attack. One day, having failed through faulty guidance to reach the place appointed for the night's halt, they bivouacked in a wood not far from Hormuz. Next morning, when they were on the point of setting out, the hot wind came down on them and stifled them all, so that no one survived to carry back the news to their lord. The men of Hormuz, hearing of this, went out to bury the corpses, so that they should not infect the air. When they gripped them by the arms to drag them to their graves, they were so parched by the tremendous heat that the arms came loose from the trunk, so that there was nothing for it but to dig the graves beside the corpses and heave them in.

After I had finished reading there was a moment's consultation, then Mr. Biluchi spoke up to say that it was the first time he had heard this particular story. But although the tale itself was new, the deadly wind was very well known. Indeed, said Mr. Biluchi, no man could live for many months in Bandar Abbas without experiencing 'Julo' the Flame, which some men called 'the breath of Kabul'. It was a notoriously fierce parching wind from the desert interior which came on certain days in May, June and July. When the Flame blew out of Baluchistan, he continued, every living creature retired to shelter until the wind was spent, for even the cooling towers were useless.

The cooling towers, to which Mr. Biluchi referred, were interesting features of the Gulf coast architecture. Each tower was like a large open chimney, some eight feet square, let directly into the roof of the more important living rooms. The principle behind these towers was the same as with a normal chimney, except that in this case there was no need for a fire. Instead, the fetid air currents at roof level drew up the stale air from the room through the wide shaft, and a cooler breeze blew in at the door to replace the loss. It was a simple but effective device for ventilation and for circulating the air in the scorching heat so that indoor life was made bearable.

I went on to ask Mr. Biluchi about the famous Hormuz date wine, concerning which Marco had written that 'In this country they made date wine with the addition of various spices, and very good it is.' In reply Mr. Biluchi sent his servant to bring a bottle of the self-same wine and some glasses. While we waited he explained to me the difference between palm toddy made from the rising sap of a freshly cut palm, and true palm wine made by steeping dates, raisins and spices in water to ferment for one month during the hot season. The making of this spirit is now strictly controlled by the Government for it can be harmful when drunk in large quantities during the hot weather, though Marco insisted that 'when it is drunk by men who are not used to it, it loosens the bowels and makes a thorough purge; but after that it does them good and makes them put on flesh'.

At the close of the day's business Mr. Biluchi invited me to spend the night at his home. As the roof was the coolest place after the sun had gone down, I contentedly curled up in the open air on an ancient Isfahan carpet, which must have been worth a small fortune. Next morning I was awoken by the arrival of the household manservants, clambering up to the roof for their dawn devotions towards Mecca. Afterwards, a larger and even more precious carpet was spread. Cushions were brought, and Mr. Biluchi with another guest appeared in elegantly flowing white gowns, which on the Gulf Coast replace the dull pyjama trousers and shirt of central Iran. The three of us sat round while servants padded back and forth bearing bowls of yoghourt, dishes of dates and scented mango. For the first time in Persia I breakfasted on a delicious combination of mint leaves rolled in bread and dipped into a mustard-coloured paste of ground nutmegs, cloves and spices mixed with lemon juice. When we were finished and the finger bowls had been cleared away, Mr. Biluchi shared a hookah with his other guest, and at my elbow appeared a fresh packet of cigarettes beside a gorgeous mother-of-pearl ashtray. Lounging back sipping Çay from a glass ceremonially presented to me in a delicately wrought silver holder with matching teaspoon, I listened contentedly to the bubbling of the water pipe. My fellow guest was a splendid study, a superb turbaned sea captain, more negro than Arab, with pierced ears and a jovial paunch. His dhow lay off the jetty and on the evening breeze he sailed for Bombay. I was invited to make the journey aboard his craft. For one moment, in that Arabian Nights' scene, I nearly forgot all about Marco Polo and accepted his offer.

But instead I went down to the bus-station, accompanied by one of Mr. Biluchi's servants. Due to his influence, I was accorded the seat of honour, next to the door, on the daily bus to Kerman. The bus followed the same road which was the third possible Polian route between Hormuz and Kerman, the lowland road around the flank of the mountains via Saidabad. But it soon became clear that this lowland route was quite out of the question as a possible Polian trail, for it did not correspond in the least with Marco's description, and could be eliminated from the practical study of his journey. The ride to Kerman was dreadfully monotonous across a parched plain only enlivened by the occasional boulder-capped earth pillar and a sparse chain of 'Beau Geste' mud forts fluttering the red, white and green of the Iranian national standard.

At Kerman I took the precaution of calling at the mission hospital to check on the condition of my broken foot which had been receiving more of a battering than it deserved. The Austrian mission doctor, who had run the hospital for many years, was intrigued by the problems of Polo's travels in the area, and he volunteered some information about the 'very fine wild asses', which Marco recorded as abundant on the road between Yezd and Kerman. These wild asses or onagers are very like yellow zebras in appearance, with the same thick necks, and today they still exist, as they have done ever since Alexander's army passed that way in the fourth century B.C. Somehow, despite failing vegetation, the wild asses manage to flourish on the fringe of the desert, though now their chief enemies are 'modern' shooting parties armed with tommy guns, hunting down the wild ass from powerful American limousines careering over the scrub. It is doubtful whether the asses will survive this slaughter for long, because they prove extremely difficult to keep in captivity. The doctor knew of one instance where a half-grown wild ass was captured and placed for the night in a corral with some tame mules. Next morning the onager had broken out, leaving behind the corpses of several mules which it had savaged to death.

From Kerman the bus took me eastward to Zahidan near the Pakistan border, where I then turned north to travel the long haul to Meshed, jumping-off point for northern Afghanistan. Whereas Marco had cut diagonally through the heart of the Great Salt Desert, the bus service is forced to skirt the eastern edge of the desert. Even so, the road is one of the worst in Persia. In summer a good deal of the day's journey must be done after nightfall because of the intense heat during the day, and we were very seldom on the road around noon. Instead, as the sun approached its zenith, the passengers would flop down apathetically in a rest-house to escape the worst heat. One day it seemed to me that the bus had been caught out in the open desert just as the sun was creeping upward to its hottest blaze. In the middle of the flat desert, without a dwelling place in sight, the bus halted like a motionless dot on the shimmering white expanse. The coachwork was far too hot to touch, and the water bubbled ominously in the radiator. The driver climbed gingerly out onto the salt crust, and we followed him to a narrow shaft dug into the ground. One by one the passengers squeezed down into the tunnel, and we found ourselves in an underground cavern. Benches and tables had been carved out of the earth, transforming the crypt into a macabre caravanserai with the atmosphere of a catacomb. A tiny hole in the roof let in a single blinding shaft of light from the desert, shining down in a solid beam as if concentrated through a powerful magnifying glass. The landlord, a solitary hermit, partially blind from desert eyesores, made his living by selling glasses of water to the rare visitors. It was difficult to imagine a more precarious existence on the boundary between life and death, already entombed below ground with a lifeless world above his head.

The bus which accomplished the worst stretch of desert was the largest, and by far the most decrepit, vehicle that I had yet ridden in. The bodywork was of a long-since outmoded style and the engine was shielded only by an old sack stretched across a length of wire. On the roof were no less than fourteen spare tyres, plus a variety of home-made spare parts. All in all, it certainly did not appear capable of crossing the desert. As I climbed aboard, my eye fell on a discreet plaque screwed to the bulkhead, and there I read this nostalgic announcement :—

> This body constructed by the Metropolitan-Cammel
> Carriage and Wagon Company Ltd.
> Birmingham, England.

Despite my misgivings, the stalwart Leyland put up a better performance than any other vehicle on the road. We shot past jeeps and private cars alike. Our driver was a miracle of skill and cool nerve, flinging the bus around the gravel curves like a racing car. Then, just as I was proudly pointing out the merits of British engineering to my fellow passengers, there was a terrific crash as the back-axle disintegrated.

Luckily it was late afternoon when we were stranded, so all the passengers clambered out and resigned themselves to sleep on the sand until a relief vehicle should turn up. Following the general example I commandeered the full-length back seat and fell fast asleep. On awaking some hours later, I was distinctly disturbed to find that I was the only living creature in the vicinity of the stranded bus. Everyone else had mysteriously abandoned the wreck and vanished with all their baggage. As there was no way of knowing what had happened or, more important, when the next vehicle would pass by along the desert road, I did not relish the prospect of enduring several days in the sea of sand with nothing but radiator water to drink. Hopping down, I peered hopefully down the track. At first light next morning there came the welcome sound of an engine, and a jeep bounced into view. I hobbled briskly forward into the road. But my weird Long John Silver appearance must have been too much of a shock for the occupants of the jeep. With startled glances, they fled past as if they had seen a peculiarly unlikely mirage. This was a blatant challenge to my ingenuity, so I scrambled back into the bus and unscrewed half a dozen seats. These I arranged across the track in a flimsy roadblock, and then sat back to await a victim. Sure enough, the second and, as I later found out, the last, jeep of the day careered to a spectacular halt in a welter of upholstery. After that, I had no difficulty in rejoining my former bus companions at the next main town, to learn that they had been picked up by a relief bus and had felt it best not to disturb the mad Inglesi when he was resting!

My fellow passengers had originally questioned my sanity during an incident on the previous evening. We had stopped after dark at a small caravanserai, and the time had come at long last for me to remove the plaster cast encasing my foot. My doctor's instructions were to bathe the swollen foot in warm salt water. Calling over the owner of the resthouse I asked him to heat some water for me in a basin. When this was ready, I requested some 'nemek' or salt. Nothing happened, except astonished looks appeared over every face in view. Thinking only that they did not see why I needed so much salt, I demanded my 'nemek' even more sternly. With a look of long-suffering patience my next-door neighbour leant over and picked up two stones from the ground. Handing them to me, he indicated that I should rub them together to supply my craving for 'nemek'. Only then did it dawn upon me that, sitting in a desert Çay–khanah, we were surrounded by a few million tons of the stuff.

One very noticeable feature about the roads near the frontiers of Persia are the chains of military roadblocks. They are set up to curtail the smuggling of such articles as radios, cigarettes, spirits, tea and luxury goods. The roadblocks themselves do not amount to much—a bored lieutenant and a small squad of militiamen nursing a diminutive spiked log laid across the road. The chief drawback of these roadblocks is the tedious waste of time entailed.

A sergeant climbs aboard and executes a desultory search. At the same time all European travellers must sign a sort of visitor's book. Some of the bus drivers object very strongly to this delay, and then a roadblock becomes tremendous fun for everyone except the perspiring soldiers. While the driver adamantly refuses to let a single soldier touch his precious bus, all the occupants pour out and gather in abusive knots round individual militiamen. The postman, who always travels by bus from village to village with a specially reserved seat, also jumps out waving his canvas post bag striped with the Iranian national colours, and shrieking that the mail must go through unhindered. Eventually the lieutenant gives way beneath this tirade, and the soldiers remove their log. With a push-start the bus coughs into motion, and then at the last critical moment, the exuberant grease-monkey leans out to crow his delight at the discomforted soldiery. With a scream of anger at this sally the sergeant sends two of his men doubling ahead to put the log down again in front of the wheels. The whole uproar then takes place all over again, the process being repeated *ad infinitum* until the soldiery are too exhausted to carry their log any farther.

With such diversions to alleviate the monotony, the Persian buses took me to the country lying north-east of the Great Desert. This is the land of Marco Polo's 'Tunocain', where grows the fabled Arbre Sec, which is 'of great size and girth. Its leaves are green on one side; white on the other. It produces husks like chestnut husks; but there is nothing in them. Its wood is hard and yellow like box wood. And there are no trees near it for 100 miles, except in one direction where there are trees ten miles away. It is here, according to the people of that country, that the battle was fought between Alexander and Darius.'

Supposedly it is also under the Arbre Sec that Alexander asked his famous question of the Gods whether or not he would become King of the World and then return safely to Macedon. Here too, a later legend more contemporary with Marco Polo, prophesied that the Arbre Sec would bloom again 'when the Pope leads the Christians to fight the Tartars and all idolators to extermination on that spot'.

It is doubtful whether Marco Polo went as far north as Meshed before crossing into Afghanistan, but he describes the area which he entered after leaving the desert as a place where 'the towns and villages enjoy great abundance of good things of every sort; for the climate is admirably tempered, neither too hot nor too cold.' This description coincides with the fertile region of low hills lying south of Meshed, a smiling green countryside which is a Promised Land after the desolation of the Dasht-i-Lut. By some it is called the Garden of Iran, and the produce of its bounty lies heaped on the stalls of Meshed, peaches, nectarines, plums, apples and other fruits. In the meanest rest-house it is possible to gorge on rich kebab soaked in egg-yolk, an unheard-of luxury farther South.

Meshed is the last main centre before the Afghan border, though there is almost no traffic across the frontier except a mail bus and perhaps two oil tankers each week. Before I left Meshed I paid a visit to the Alley of the Goldsmiths in the central bazaar and converted my Persian tumans into gold sovereigns. Armed with these as a safeguard against cruelly unfair 'official' rates of exchange I caught a local bus to the border. Unfortunately I had missed the weekly connection to Herat in Afghanistan and was forced to hitch a lift in a dusty staff car taking an officer to the frontier garrison. As we bumped along, this officer lectured me on the iniquities of the smuggling link between Afghanistan and Iran— well-mounted horsemen slipping through the hills to carry hashish into Persia in exchange for gold which is jealously hoarded by the Afghans. As the penalty for this traffic is death, it was just as well that my companion remained oblivious to the chink of gold coins coming from my own pocket. As it was, when we reached the border, my acquaintanceship with the officer produced a smooth passage through the control posts and with a feeling of relief I found myself aboard an oil tanker driving through Afghanistan to Herat.

10

AFGHANISTAN

THE EXACT PATH of Marco Polo's route through Northern
Afghanistan will always remain a puzzle until, perhaps, fresh details about his journey are discovered so that a more accurate
picture can be built up. The chief difficulty in locating Marco's
trail springs from the exceptionally vague account which he gives
of his wanderings along that particular stage of his journey.

This may be because Marco Polo was too ill at that time to make
many notes on his surroundings, for one version of the Travels
states that 'Messer Marco fell ill in these parts for a year'. Despite
these gaps in the narrative, certain valid interpolations can be
made.

It is obvious that any caravan coming up out of the low-lying
saltpans of the Dasht-i-Lut must sooner or later reach the waters
of the Hari Rud. Where this river drains westward out of the
splayed fingers of the Hindu Kush, its valley widens out to form a
natural corridor. The focal point of activity in this East-West
passageway is the ancient city of Herat, situated where the Hari
Rud debouches from the hill country. From Herat the caravan
trails lead due east upstream to Kabul, north-east over saddle
passes in the Paropamisus to Balkh and Samarkand, west to Persia
and northward to the Turkmen Karakum. As far back as the
fourth century B.C. Alexander the Great had recognized the key
location of Herat and founded there a city, 'Alexandria of the
Arians', before turning south on a fruitless venture into Drangiana.

The Polo caravan must have passed within a few miles of this world-famous metropolis. Yet Marco never even mentions its existence. The reason for this surprising omission is to be found in the appalling devastation which was left behind in the wake of the Chingizide invasions. Some forty years before Polo's visit, an army of 80,000 warriors under Genghis Khan had crossed the Oxus and laid siege to Herat. For six months the city survived until the fateful day when the exasperated Mongol horde broke through the walls to massacre and obliterate. When the last embers of Herat's funeral pyre grew cold, scarcely forty humans out of the city's million and a half inhabitants were left alive. Genghis, with a 'magazine of warriors' at his back, poured down upon the carcass of Persia, and behind him the entire province lay prostrate at the shock of his passing. Thus, even when the Polo family journeyed peacefully along the trade route through the valley, there could have been nothing worth noting down in the caravan's journal except the existence of a few timid peasants cowering like animals in their lairs between pitiful attempts to reconstruct the essentials of their humble existence.

The route which Alexander marched is still in use, and in high summer the valley of the Shari Rud winds along in a ribbon of fertility. The gravel track out of Persia twists around the low bluffs, crowned with small hamlets. The river flats are dotted with great herds of camels, plunging belly-deep in the tall grasses. Occasionally the road cuts across the steppe-like upper plain, and the thunder of one's vehicle sends clusters of bulbuls scurrying into the air on quick wing-beats. At one point the main trail curls across the river by way of an ancient whale-backed bridge, straddling the shallows in a series of half-choked sunbaked arches each as old as time. In such parts of Afghanistan the traveller, as he journeys along the traditional routes, is pressed about with a heavy feeling of untouched history.

But in Herat itself the magic of the countryside is lost. The modern city has little to boast about. It hovers uncertainly between past glories and modern progress. On the one hand the walled courtyards flaunt an air of graceful decay. On the other, Russian built lorries rumble past horse-taxis garnished with plastic flowers. Even the gaudy turbans of the hawk-faced hillmen are made of nylon net. Everywhere Russian technicians are easily recognizable, for this is a Russian sphere of influence, and the foreigners go clothed in their regulation dress of panama hat and baggy cotton suits. In the bazaar the Russian wives, equally uniformed in print dresses and head-scarves, barter for their household needs with grim efficiency and fluent Afghan. This is a source of much chagrin to the stall-holders, for it is difficult to out-argue a fifteen stone engineer's wife who has very definite ideas about her weekly budget.

Every foreigner on entering Herat must register immediately at the Police Headquarters. There a plain-clothes police official thumbs through one's papers and states that the normal tourist permit is only valid for two weeks. On his desk are stacked neat blocks of bright, unsullied Russian passports, their untarnished lettering contrasting significantly with the faded blue covers of the very occasional British passport. The Russians, however, were not obliged to make a personal appearance to prove their identity.

The policeman seemed to find it hard to believe that I had no definite plans in Afghanistan except to rejoin Stan and Mike in order to follow the trail of some long-dead traveller. Tourists were unwelcome in Herat, for they constituted a nuisance to an already harassed police department. Worst of all, I was immediately forbidden to travel to Kabul along the Northern motor road. This was a bitter blow, for this northerly route is the nearest equivalent to Marco Polo's trail. In the eyes of officialdom the safest way of dealing with unwanted visitors was to hand them on as swiftly as possible to the capital, where such pests really belong. As a further precaution the Police Captain allocated me an 'interpreter', whose English was as bad as my Afghan, but who was more interested in following me about than helping out with any language problems.

It is only natural that a footloose stranger should be placed under surveillance by the Police, and certainly the gendarmerie were only doing their duty. Yet somehow the unwavering attention of an over-officious escort grew increasingly irritating. For one thing, it was now impossible to get rid of the gold that I had brought in with me from Persia. Even closer to the bone was the unhappy arrangement with the horse-taxis. As my foot was still troubling me I could not walk very far, and every time I hailed one of the gigs my faithful shadow would appear at my elbow.

The moment I scrambled aboard, my escort nimbly hopped in after me, and when I gave the driver his directions, my ideas would swiftly be over-ruled by my travelling companion, so that we clattered off to a more suitable area of interest, as defined by his professional choice. In the end the path of our severely curtailed jaunt would loop back and terminate, as if by chance, outside the half-constructed shell of the Herat Hotel. At that point my escort would blandly suggest that what I really needed was a good long rest.

After this pantomime had been enacted three or four times, I got heartily fed up with the unequal rules of the game, and most of all with having to pay the double fare for my unwanted companion. The final circuit proved longer and more expensive than the earlier ones, so when we drew up outside the hotel once again, I took the opportunity to slip smartly indoors, leaving my inscrutable sleuth the unhappy task of paying off the avaricious taxi man. While my guardian argued over the fare, I slunk out of the hotel by the back exit and set off to appreciate the more attractive and less official aspects of Herat.

The hub of the city was the bazaar, and in this respect Herat was once again the great mart. On the open sites surrounding the market area were large disorderly camel trains; the camels slumped haughtily between the piles of wares, while their owners haggled over the cost of taking the goods into the little hill-village markets. The bazaar centre was formed by a sprawling network of narrow alleys, each alley devoted to some specialized product. The clashing and banging in the coppersmiths' alley and the smell of kebab roasting on thin skewers over the charcoal braziers, was no different to the markets of either Isfahan or far Istanbul. The special characteristic of Herat's bazaar, which made it uniquely Afghan, centred upon the dozens and dozens of karakul merchants. The doorways of their shops were hung with great bunches of semi-cured fleeces taken from very young lambs. Inside, the shelves were lined with the characteristic pill-box hats of Afghanistan, made in the crisp curly karakul wool, dyed silver, black or brown. On a central bench were more hats, taking shape around wooden forms, for a really smart cap must be shrunk to the exact shape of the wearer's head.

Sharing the alleys of karakul merchants were the shops of the skin merchants. Their doorways were decorated with dangling pelts of mountain leopards, though the main business centred around the splendid skins of full-grown Afghan sheep. The luxuriant wool on these fleeces hung like massed fibres of soft white silk, each strand combed to three or four inches in length. After they had been dressed, the skins could be shaped into rugs, mittens, waistcoats and soft slippers with curly toes.

Above all, the very finest fleeces went to make the magnificent winter jackets of the high plateau, where the temperature stays below freezing point for months on end. The natural fleece lining of these jackets hangs in thick warm fronds which are proof against the most bitter weather and the garment is cut so that the sleeves extend well past the finger tips and the skirts reach over the thighs. On the more fancy winter coats the outside skin is also dyed in brilliant colours and then decorated with silver braid or with thread, a status symbol for its owner.

Wandering unescorted through the bazaar's twisting back-streets, I could sense a marked difference in the atmosphere of the market. There was something which was strangely new and which, for a short while, I was unable to pin-point. Then quite suddenly it dawned on me that in this, unlike the bazaars of Turkey and Persia, I was not a public gazing stock. For once, the crowd did not stop to stare in idle curiosity at the strange foreigner. The Afghans neither shewed obvious interest nor did they push and prod, as other people had done. In the market of Herat the passers-by gave me a single level glance and then moved on with uncon-cerned dignity. It was an uncanny sensation after months of tire-some attention from local crowds.

Calling in at a local Çay-khaneh where the air smelt strongly of hashish, it was strange to sit down and order a pot of thin, clear tea in surroundings of quiet indifference. The presence of a wandering stranger went unheeded and life carried on normally in the resthouse. It was time to prepare the evening meal for the customers later in the day, and the cook was busy slaughtering one of that famous breed of fat-tailed Afghan sheep, which Marco had described as: 'big as an ass with tails so thick and plump that they weigh a good thirty pounds. Fine fat beasts they are, and good eating.' The pendulous slab of a tail certainly seems odd to Western eyes, a reminder of medieval fables about sheep whose

tails were so fat and heavy that they had to be dragged along behind them on special trolleys as the flocks grazed.

The actual technique of converting a bawling, frightened ram
into the greasy evening stew was an education in practical dexterity. A knife thrust into a neck vein neatly despatched the animal.
Then, completely unconcerned at my obvious interest, the cook
cut a small slit in the skin near a hind hoof, and placing his lips
against the gash, began to inflate the hide with long, steady breaths.
Gradually the carcass began to bloat like a limp balloon, and
another helper took over the task of inflating the dead sheep. When
the carcass was considered to be ready, a slicing dagger stroke
punctured the skin and disembowelled the animal in one movement. Then the skin was peeled smoothly off like a loose stocking,
for the blowing exercise had literally blown the skin off the animal
by forcing a layer of air between the membrane and the undam-
aged flesh. The main stomach gut was carefully squeezed out and
put aside for later use, and the raw carcass was abruptly hacked up
and tossed into the cauldron. The whole process had taken little
more than ten minutes from start to finish.

Unhappily, officialdom was not prepared to let me enjoy an
unlimited stay in Herat, and when I eventually got back to the
hotel I was informed that I had to be on the next plane to Kabul.
There was just time to send a cable to Stan and Mike c/o the
British Embassy in Kabul, warning them of my precipitate arrival,
though I had no idea of where, in all Eurasia, my two companions
had got to. Fortunately the telephone service in Afghanistan is
superb, even if the roads are poor and railways non-existent. The
country's telephone wire run like vital nerve systems, connecting
one town with the next. At first I had constantly been surprised
how well the local police were informed about tourists, but later
I learned that in nearly every case the vital intelligence had been
passed on by telephone.

At the Post office I came across three American surveyors working under a Foreign Aid programme, who had come north into
the Russian zone to pick up their supplies and mail. After the usual
greetings I was flabbergasted to be informed that three days
earlier and five hundred miles farther south, these same Americans
had encountered two other young Englishmen wearing motorcycle jackets and boots. Without a doubt Stan and Mike had been

sighted, and with this stroke of good fortune I knew the exact whereabouts of my colleagues for the first time since they had left me at the hospital in Teheran.

In fact, this mysterious Oriental grapevine of rumour and hear-say, unknown to me, had also been working in reverse, supplying Stan and Mike with a steady stream of information about my own movements. In Kerman and elsewhere, awestruck villagers told them that a mad, lone Inglesi had been seen leaving for the hills astride a camel, some said a donkey. He was a cripple, they reported, and carried crutches strapped across his back. It was enchanting how tales like these magnified and acquired glamour by repetition, for I too remembered one splendid encounter with a distraught oil prospector. He had been very upset because no-body would believe him when he solemnly related how, as he drove his jeep over the desert, two weird figures had swept into view over a sand dune. The phantom travellers, he insisted, rode astride a battered motorcycle, which went roaring past at a suicidal speed and vanished as mysteriously as it had appeared. I had not the heart to destroy so vivid a mystery with a prosaic explanation.

In some cases in the East rumours seem to fly faster and more reliably than the scheduled air services. For three days I waited morosely in the shade of a jeep in Herat's airstrip, while the driver hopefully twiddled the knobs of his ground-to-air radio, or more intelligently, listened for the sound of approaching airplane engines. Even my faithful police watchdog began to shew signs of irritated boredom, while for my own part, I plunged happily into my fast developing hobby of controlled sleeping.

There can scarcely be a more necessary part of the lone Oriental traveller's physique than the ability to control his own waking and sleeping. Once this vital skill has been acquired, it becomes a fathomless source of interest, relaxation and entertainment. The knack of doing this comes quite suddenly after a long, arduous apprenticeship of frustrated tedium. Whereas a European regrets a single wasted hour, the Persian or Afghan can calmly accept a dull and totally uneventful year. In many situations the Western visitor is in no position to speed up the languid local time-scale. If a plane is a week late, or a truck breaks down in the mountains miles from help, there is nothing more edifying than to turn over and go to sleep until something else turns up. Although this attitude fringes on fatalism, it is a form of fatalism mingled with appreciation. When no cushions or mattresses are needed, any rock or bundle makes a comfortable pillow and a threadbare carpet is more luxurious than down-filled bedding. With time, the sleeper slowly returns to his primitive state. Like an animal, he learns to fall asleep immediately and wake up clear-headed after a brief ten minutes or twenty hours of complete relaxation. At its best, this brand of controlled sleeping becomes a magic lantern, exchanging the meanest dull surroundings for a gentle haven of relaxation.

Afghanistan can test the art of controlled sleeping more than most other countries. The land itself has been asleep for many years, and it seems a pity that it must soon wake up. Flashes of the old way of life survive, and no occidental can legitimately demand that everything should run to precise schedules. The exacting pace of the twentieth century rules in Kabul, the capital, but life is more leisurely in the provinces. No one expects the weekly aeroplane to arrive until its engines are heard droning through the sky. The aircraft only stays for a quarter of an hour before it turns round to leave, and what is a mere fifteen minutes in all the history of Herat.

In the end the long-awaited aircraft did arrive, and joining the little huddle of grave-faced Afghan elders in their baggy robes, we clambered aboard and settled into the scuffed seats of a very tired Dakota belonging to Ariana, Royal Afghan Airways. With only a brief fuelling stop at Kandahar, the plane flew over the monotonous arid interior of the country, the yellow curves of the sandstone hills slipping drearily past beneath our wings. Occasionally the Dakota ran into turbulent air currents spiralling off the hot desert below, and we shook, heaved and bounced spectacularly. At such moments, several of my solemn travelling companions gravely removed their turbans and, still maintaining absolute dignity, vomited into the up-turned folds.

At last the aircraft dropped lower and we snaked a precarious path between the mountain slopes that surround Kabul. From the bleak airfield I rode a smart German-made bus into the city, and at the Turkish Embassy I found Stan and Mike camping at the back of the Chancery building. We celebrated our re-union in a

Çay–khanah near the bazaar and after having exchanged news about our independent wanderings, took stock of our current situation.

For the moment we had a base in Kabul, as the Turkish Ambassador to Afghanistan, whom we had originally met some thousands of miles away in Istanbul, had invited us to stay with him. Probably, as a diplomat, he had not expected to be taken at his word, nor had he considered it likely that our madcap venture would ever reach Kabul. Unfortunately for him, we arrived in time to accept his hospitality, however meagre, and seeing how the land lay, we were determined to rub in the value of genuine help rather than oily niceties.

From this reluctant foster-home our main purpose was to visit the Forbidden Corridor of the Wakhan, which forms a narrow north-eastern appendix of Afghanistan along the upper Oxus, running out in a long, thin tongue between Russia, China and Pakistan. Unfortunately we were faced with the virtually impossible task of obtaining official permission to enter this Corridor which is strictly closed to all strangers. Our slim chances of obtaining such permission were made even less hopeful by the tension at that time between Afghanistan and Pakistan over their common frontier in the Pathan tribal areas. Another point we had to tackle was that we still had no idea how the Marco Polo Route Project was going to get back to England. The University Year began in three weeks, and between us we mustered £40 and one very exhausted motorcycle.

This unhappy machine was in a state of near-collapse. All the lights had long since been shattered; the front brake functioned only very feebly, while the rear brake did not work at all; the gear lever had been snapped off; both wheels, as well as the handlebars, were badly out of alignment, and the shock-absorbers were partially disintegrated. The once proud BSA had been thrashed into a foul mass of dust, dents, and miscellaneous pieces of grass rope holding it together. In order to change gear, the agile driver was forced to bend over and rummage around by his right foot for the sheered-off stub of the gear lever. To slow down, the passenger had to assist by dragging his feet in the dust, and at any speed the cracked steering arms exuded a fine spray of oil. The only consolation was that with the machine in such a decrepit condition there was no likelihood of it being stolen, for Stan was the only person who had the strength, experience and foolhardiness to coax the wreck into motion.

Having taken stock of our situation, we decided that Mike and Stan should go on the motorcycle to visit the Lakes of Band-i-Amir and Great Buddha at Bamian, about ninety miles west of Kabul. In the meantime my injured foot would have a further chance to get stronger in preparation for some more motorcycling. While Stan and Mike were away on their excursion, I was to approach the Afghan authorities for permission to enter the Wakhan Corridor, and there would be time for me to cable my brother in England to find out whether, as the expedition's Home Agent, he could arrange to get us back to England in time for University commitments.

From the first, it was evident that we would not be allowed into the Forbidden Wakhan Corridor. The frontier quarrel with Pakistan was far too tense. Even so I spent several days waiting in Government offices. Only the King or the Prime Minister could give the necessary permission, and both men were unapproachable because of the political crisis. My sole consolation was that the American Ambassador had just returned from a hunting trip in the Wakhan, and he was able to describe to me the fabulous Ovis Poli, the great horned sheep of the High Pamir. These magnificent creatures had not been seen for six centuries after Marco Polo described them in his Journal, and when the great sheep had once again been located in their remote mountain fastnesses, they were named in honour of the famous Venetian who first described them to the Western World. Today the awesome spread of horns that the rams use for mating battles and defence against wolves and bears, is a major hunting trophy, but the best description is still Marco's

> There are great quantities of sheep of a huge size. Their horns grow to as much as six palms in length and are never less than three or four. From these horns the shepherds make big bowls from which they feed, and also fences to keep in their flocks. There are also innumerable wolves, which devour many of the wild rams. The horns and bones of these sheep are found in such great numbers that men build cairns of them beside the tracks to serve as landmarks to travellers in the snowy season.

It was frustrating to think that we could not see these magnificent creatures after following Polo so far. Some day I hope the Afghan authorities will be able to grant us permission to visit the Forbidden Corridor where 'No birds fly because of the height and the cold. And because of the very great cold, the fire is not so bright nor does it burn with the usual colour, but does not cook so well.'

Meanwhile, Stan and Mike were at least seeing part of Marco's 'rich province of Badakshan', where, according to him, the horses were once descended from Alexander's Bucephalus and there are three mountains, one of rubies, one of sapphire, and one of lapis lazuli, but they were Royal monopolies where 'no one else might go to dig for these gems without incurring instant death, and it is further forbidden under pain of death and forfeiture to export them out of the Kingdom.'

On their way to Bamian through this southern portion of Badakshan, Mike and Stan rode north to Charikar, and then turned westward off the metalled road into the Chardeh valley, one of the loveliest parts of Afghanistan. The lofty mountains on each side bear the magic name of the Hindu Kush and the river foams its path between them in a land where Marco says:

> The mountains are of immense height, so that for a man to climb from the bottom to the top is a full day's journey, from dawn till dusk. On top are wide plateaux, with a lush growth of grass and trees and copious springs of the purest water, which pour down over the crags like rivers into the valleys below. In these streams are found trout and other choice fish. On the mountain tops the air is so pure and salubrious that if a man living in the cities and houses built in the adjoining valleys falls sick of a fever, whether tertian, quartan, or hectic, he has only to go up into the mountains, and a few days' rest will banish the malady and restore him to health.

As Stan and Mike rode deeper into the Chardeh valley, the real Afghanistan began to unfold itself, quiet little villages near small pockets of meadow land, and scattered flocks of sheep moving against the steep rocky hillsides. In the hayfields the villagers squatted in lines to cut handfuls of mountain grass with short bill hooks. Behind them, their womenfolk stooped to gather the wispy hanks of hay and pile the tufts into heaps to be dried by wind and sun. Then the harvest is carried home in great stacks aboard the tiny donkeys, so that it seems as if flotillas of restless haystacks are trotting of their own accord to the village store house.

This is the land of the 'kochi' tribes, the true Afghan nomads, who roam the land in their tribal groups. In summer and winter they follow the pasture for their herds, wherever it may be found The kochi bands wander at will, obeying only the natural laws and the rules of their own tribe. Often they cross the border to spend the winter on the warmer slopes of Pakistan. Each tribesman carries his accoutrements, curved daggers, crossed bandoliers, and carefully tended rifle slung over one shoulder. Independence is their creed, and as Marco Polo put it; 'they are an exceptionally warlike people,' whose women 'in one pair of trousers or breeches put anything up to a hundred ells of cotton cloth, folded in pleats. This is to give the impression that they have plump thighs, because their menfolk delight in plumpness.'

All along the gravel track of the Chardeh valley Stan and Mike ran across groups of these fierce nomads moving round the bluffs with their long straggles of camels. In front and at strategic intervals along the column stalked the warriors. The womenfolk led the ladened camels, and all but the tiniest children scurried on bare feet along the line of march. Just such caravans could have shuffled their way straight from the pages of Marco Polo's Journal or from the illuminated illustrations of medieval fantasies about the Orient.

Naturally Mike could not resist filming such a pageant and once, having just passed one such 'kochi' camel train, he asked Stan to halt. Scrambling up the hillside to a strategic vantage-point for his camera tripod, Mike shouted at Stan to go back down the road and re-appear round the bluff, picturesquely weaving his way between the camels. Stan fulfilled his instructions with enormous verve, and the roaring motorcycle sent the camels shying wildly up the hillside with their desperate owners dangling helplessly from the halters. But Mike was not satisfied. Stan had swept into view too soon, and as far as the photographer was concerned, the film was not up to his own standards. Stan was obliged to re-enact the scene, only this time the nomads had wearied of the sport and knew precisely what to expect. As Stan sped round the corner, he was greeted with a hail of stones and sticks. With these projectiles whistling around his crash helmet, Stan weaved nimbly through the enemy ranks, ducking low over the handlebars to dodge the occasional up-raised menace of a jagged rock, wielded by an irate nomad. As far as the film was involved, the brisk adventure was superb material, but Mike was enraged. His job was to produce a good film of the trip, and he had a very low opinion of anyone who interfered with him in his chosen work.

Leaping back down to the roadway, where Stan stood astride the motorcycle, nervously revving the engine for a quick getaway, Mike scorned the idea of retreat. Stalking past Stan, who had no doubts that a swift departure was the order of the day, Mike tucked his camera under his arm and strode down the road towards the advance guard of the heavily armed nomads who now appeared like a swarm of angry bees. Mike's lone figure stamped forward. Incredulously, as Mike closed with them, the tribal vanguard faltered. Hands clutched warily at the hilts of daggers and tribesmen closed in around the solitary European. Totally oblivious to any danger Mike selected the chieftain of the group and caught hold of him by a bandolier. Then, thrusting his camera under the beak nose of his astonished victim, Mike delivered a blistering harangue on the ethics of interfering with a film cameraman in the execution of his duty. A wondering murmur swept through the nomad ranks at this totally incomprehensible flood of Cockney invective, delivered with enough facial grimaces to make the basic idea clear to even the meanest intelligence. With stabbing, emphatic sign language Mike explained that he would film what he liked, when he liked, and where he liked. Then, to Stan's amazement, Mike ordered the motorcycle to drive through the caravan once again, while the bewildered warriors were shoved and pushed around like so many sheep in order that Mike could film to the best advantage.

After this episode with the nomads, Stan and Mike reached the settlement at Bamian. There, carved out of the red sandstone of the sheer valley wall, tower two enormous statues of Buddha. The twin colossi are cut into vast cavities in the cliff face, the largest one soaring up for 174 feet. The curious visitor can climb up a long chain of stairs hollowed into the cliff, and come out on the very crown of the head of the tallest Buddha. The vault of the arch above the niche is carved with crumbling frescoes to ornament the surroundings of the Most High. In front, and away before the sightless gaze of the two giant gods, stretches the panorama which has endured since the days of the sixth century A.D. when a devout colony of troglodyte Buddhists had laboured in their haven to reproduce the dominating theme of their dedicated lives.

That night the two travellers at last reached their final objective, the fabled rainbow lakes of Band-i-Amir. This series of lakes is amongst the highest in the world. In the clear air of the Hindu Kush, they lie like a broken ribbon of glowing tortoiseshell, caught between the peaks. The walls of the surrounding cliffs contract and expand, giving strange and beautiful shapes to the cold, clear waters which lie in basins, slivers and goblets of crystal. At one end of the chain, a gentle trickle flows in to feed the series. At the lower end, the same trickle re-appears,'lapping gently out over a natural dam of rock. Where this outflow spills away over the downstream face of the dam, the mineral deposits from the sheet of water have covered the rock wall with a glowing patina of mingling tints, reds, blacks and yellows. In the heady air of the high plateau with the snow-sheathed peaks gleaming at a romantic distance, the limpid purity of the lakes of Band-i-Amir with their sheen of many colours successfully isolate an unsullied shrine of beauty.

Fascinated by this charming landscape Stan and Mike overstayed their schedule. Daybreak on the following morning saw them started on the long ride back to Kabul. By dint of hard driving along the river road they covered most of the return road by daylight, but it was the early hours of the following morning when they finally reached the capital.

Meanwhile, I had been busily hastening around Kabul, arranging the next leg of the Marco Polo Route Project. We had to accept that our journey in the actual footsteps of Marco was now suspended. Our ambitions for the Wakhan Corridor or a visit to China must wait until the relevant authorities were kind enough to give us the vital official permission without which such journeys were impossible. Now, our only alternative route out of Kabul and Afghanistan lay through the Khyber Pass into Pakistan and the Indian sub-continent. Once we left Kabul, our trip would become no more than a gratification of the tourist's wish, for we left Polo's route behind us. The immediate problem was that even the Khyber Route was by no means certain. The Pushtoonistan crisis was heading for a severance of diplomatic relations between Afghanistan and Pakistan, and one morning the entire Pakistan embassy was evacuated from Kabul aboard a fleet of lorries. During these days, while Stan and Mike were at Bamian and the Great Buddhas, I shuttled between Embassies, cheap hotels and police stations, trying to maintain a close watch on diplomatic developments and the provision of our exist visas.

These short journeys between the various points of information proved to be ruinously expensive, for my foot was giving me trouble and I had to travel by horse taxi. Very soon I found myself obliged to visit the moneylenders in the bazaar in order to change into Afghanis the gold coins that I had brought with me from Persia. As I haggled over the rate of exchange for my gold, a very dejected-looking policeman wandered in to ask for a small loan. The moneylender could only offer a fantastically high rate of interest, and the sad policeman began to look even more miserable. Seizing this heaven-sent opportunity, I pointed to his official police bicycle propped up against the alley wall, and offered to lend him the money myself without interest. In exchange he could loan me his bicycle for the week. A moment later I was pedalling merrily on my way astride a new steed, while its owner contentedly counted his unexpected wealth. From that time on, whenever I passed the bicycle's owner as he was on point duty, I had to dismount while he examined the condition of his property and the rest of the traffic unhesitatingly snarled itself into knots.

When Stan and Mike eventually got back to Kabul, I was able to tell them that our passages back home to England had been arranged. A combination of my brother's efficiency as Home Agent and the great generosity of the P. & O. Company had resulted in the booking of three berths for us on one of their homebound liners. We had rather more than three weeks before we had to board the ship at Bombay.

We spent several carefree days at the Festival of Jeshyn in Kabul. The celebrations of Jeshyn in the capital of Afghanistan is one of the few occasions when the ancient and the modern aspects of the country can be seen side by side. During the festival, which celebrates the country's independence and, incidentally, its successful rejection of British imperialism, the tribesmen come down from the hills to take part in the festivities. The wild nomads from the outback on their yearly visit to the town provide traditional singing and dancing on the main showground where in the evening the city's entire population is to be found. The tribesmen in their traditional garb of loose shirt, pantaloons, turban and embroidered waistcoat, dip and swirl to the fierce stammer of the tribal drums. The dancers judder from side to side with hard stamping steps and punctuate their movements with slashing sweeps of their long black hair. Eventually the sound and fury of the drummers grows to a crescendo until only the finest dancer is left writhing out the tempo, before he too falls exhausted.

Within sight of this ancient culture rise the show-pieces of the new Afghanistan. Along one side of the fairground were exhibition pavilions built by the Government or by nations who provide the country with aid from abroad. Britain had no representation at Kabul, but Russia and the United States vied with each other to impress the visitors to the capital. The scales were heavily weighed in favour of the USSR. Inside their hall the organizers had achieved a subtle combination of all that appealed to the Afghan. Mingled with the displays of tractors and farm equipment were splendid carpets woven in the Soviet Union and for the crowd's entertainment there were folk singers from the Central Asian Republics. These and similar displays, the humble Afghan could appreciate and wonder at. Finally, with great effect, the huge façade of the hall shewed a giant rocket sweeping on its way to the stars past the smiling faces of Krushchev and Gagarin.

The festival of Jeshyn with its smells, crowds and movement, was a fitting last glimpse of Afghanistan, and when the festival was over the three of us left for the Khyber Pass. We loaded up the wretched motorcycle with three sweaters, a single toothbrush and the camera equipment, which was all the equipment we had room for. Stan straddled the petrol tank and seized the controls. Mike hopped aboard the pillion seat, and I climbed up onto the luggage frame over the rear wheel. The rear shock absorbers sank to their position of absolute loading, and I wriggled a spare inner tube under me to make the luggage grille a little more comfortable. Stan revved the engine, let in the clutch, and with a wobble or

two the Marco Polo Route Project moved out of Kabul, three on
one motorcycle.

Our route took us past the picturesque mud forts that guard
the Western approaches to the Khyber and by the time we
emerged at Peshawar, we had become quite expert at our new and
bizarre form of transport. We had begun our journey from Oxford
in style, and we determined to conclude the adventure with similar
panache. By all accounts three passengers aboard one weary
motorcycle was not to be recommended, even for short journeys.
Yet we survived all the way from Kabul to Calcutta, sweeping
our majestic way along the Grand Trunk Road, through Rawal-
pindi, Dehli and Benares. We gaped happily at the Taj Mahal and
the Golden Temple of Amritsar. In Peshawar the Brigadier of the
Frontier Constabulary arranged a superb demonstration of tribal
dancing for us, and everywhere we enjoyed ourselves hugely in
our new role as tourists.

Along the way Stan weaved the BSA between water-
buffaloes, taxis, jeeps, lorries, cyclists and pedestrians. If we looked
sideways at our racing shadows, we saw three black figures silhou-
etted by the sun; three pairs of boots stood on the footrests; and
from the front Stan must have appeared like some weird native
god with no less than six arms wavering out at different angles.
Whenever we sped towards an officious policeman on traffic duty,
Mike and I were forced to crouch in ambush behind Stan's broad
back. Then, as soon as it was too late for us to be halted, our two
extra heads would pop out grinning delightedly at the policeman's
look of astonishment.

The retreat of the monsoon that year was very delayed, and on
leaving Delhi we found that sections of the Grand Trunk Road had
been cut by heavy flooding. By then it took more than a flooded
road to halt our progress. If we found the machine submerging
into the flood water, we turned the motorcycle towards the railway
line which paralleled our route. There, on the embankment above
the swirling muddy waters, we bumped our way uncomfortably
along the sleepers of the track. Stan concentrated on manhandling
the machine over the excruciating rhythm of the sleepers. The
middle passenger looked ahead into the driving rain, and the rear
rider peered back down the track for the first sight of an express
train rushing down the rails. If anything suspicious was seen, the

look-out shouted a warning, Stan sent the motorcycle leaping over the rails, and we tumbled down the embankment like three shot rabbits.

For three thousand miles we roared our way across the Indian sub-continent. We were nearing the end of our journey and we had proved that our wild escapade in the footsteps of Marco Polo was a practical possibility. It was true that we had failed to enter the Wakhan Corridor or China, but these things could wait until another day. We had left Oxford with two motorcycles and two side-cars, and returned to Europe with a heap of misused ironmongery on wheels which a scrap merchant would hardly have bothered to take off our hands. We owed a great debt to the many people who had supported us with their help, time and advice, but at least we had in some measure repaid the confidence they had shewn in our initiative.

Most of all there was a debt to Marco Polo himself. Without his example constantly before us we would not have enjoyed a quarter of our experiences across Eurasia. Standing on the dock-side at Bombay as our motorcycle was hoisted aboard ship trailing a woebegone trickle of oil, we hoped that we had played our part by helping to prove the honest accuracy of Marco's medieval tale and done justice to the spirit of the Great Venetian.

REFLECTIONS

THE SEA VOYAGE back to England was an opportunity for
the three members of the Marco Polo Route Project to review
their trip. We had time to evaluate our experiences and to decide
what changes we would recommend for similar journeys in the
future. Inevitably our opinions differed between our various
characters and interests; so that we attached varying degrees of
importance to our many experiences. But one thing was certain;
all three of us if asked to go through the entire adventure again,
would leap at the chance without any hesitation whatsoever. This
feeling was the ultimate judgement of our trip from a purely
personal outlook, and at the same time reflected the basic unity
between our temperaments.

It is very difficult to analyse the traits of character which help
one most during a journey similar to our Eurasian crossing. To
begin with, every trip poses peculiar problems and circumstances
of its own, which in turn demand different solutions. Perhaps the
real secret of human behaviour in the face of these difficulties lies
much deeper than the usual advocacy of determination and enter-
prize. At the heart of the matter the challenges of backwoods
travel are so varied that a universal solution must be based upon
an underlying acceptance of any hazards as mere fluctuations in
the natural order of events. In this, there must be a sharp distinction between a European party ensconced securely in a four wheel
vehicle which moves like a cloud across the face of the land, and

one or two individuals hitch-hiking or motorcycling amongst the humdrum events of an exotic community. For the Land-Rover group driving from caravanserai to caravanserai along the beaten roads, this problem of acceptance does not arise, for the local difficulties are cushioned by companionship and material comforts.

By contrast the solitary traveller can survive only by going around with his eyes shut or by keeping sage counsel with himself. The first possibility is a tragedy because blind isolation wastes the precious opportunities for savouring and learning from one's surroundings. The second course of quiet appreciation is more delicate. It requires a cautious balance between wide-eyed critical detachment and complete immersion in the temporary environment. The secret of the compromise lies with the ability to maintain one's customary ease of spirit. If this is possible, then every fresh experience can be measured against a stable criterion, one's natural unbiassed reactions. At the same time there is little risk of becoming bored and dulled by new events, for any person contemplating such a trip must surely be eager to enjoy the unusual.

In fact the greatest need for any traveller seems to be some inborn talent for being on the spot when unusual events take place, or the ability to make such things happen. In the same way that two people can cross the same stretch of country and remember it in two entirely opposing impressions, two travellers can cover an identical route where one person has a totally uneventful trip while his partner is involved in all manner of fascinating escapades. In this way the Marco Polo Route Project was extraordinarily lucky, for the essential Polian theme of our journey took us away from the beaten track and into the unexpected. Furthermore we had not one, but two viewpoints. On the one hand we discovered new outlandish places where our path led us and were rewarded with fresh scenes and unlikely events. Yet, on the other hand, we would find a deeper appreciation in the comparison between our own observations and the descriptions of Marco Polo's Journal. Out of this we gained a whole new perspective to enjoy, judge and value.

One of the results of this link with Polo, made stronger not only by unchanging geography but also by the hardships which were shared to some measure over the centuries, was a finer understanding of Marco himself. Although his main writing was devoted to China and her culture, there is sufficient material in his account of the Eurasian journey to reveal something about the author himself. Following Polo's narrative along the same paths it was impossible not to see Marco in rather a different light to the academic authorities poring over their carefully annotated manuscripts. To begin with, it was easy for us to assess why Marco Polo had not provided more details about the everyday life of the lands he crossed. Part of the reason must be that the life of a medieval Persian or Afghan peasant was basically little different to the life of his contemporary European serf. Industrialization had not yet created the present contrasts and Polo did not waste words describing the commonplace. A far greater reason for this silence about social conditions must be ascribed to the monotony of Asian life. From the Bosporus to the High Pamirs the lives of ordinary people have always been ruled by the common factors of climate and terrain. The changes from one region to another are only very gradual, so that over the breadth of the Middle East everyday life is necessarily very similar. From Lesser Armenia to Badakshan the steady rhythm of existence lulls the slow caravan into unquestioning acceptance of the environment which makes comment seem trivial.

By contrast the sort of details which Marco did provide are precisely those which we ourselves came to remember : a high mountain pass, the manner of dress, local curiosities like wild asses or strange fruit, these are the vivid singularities which stay in the memory of a traveller. In the same way, Oriental legends like the Old Man of the Mountains were tailor-made for their appeal to a credulous Rialto audience. Obviously the mercantile interest too is present when Marco talks of buckram and the trade of Hormuz, but once again he tends to remember the exotic novelty of pistachio and lapis lazuli rather than the humdrum bulk of wheat and cloth which formed the main staple of trade goods along the caravan trails.

Having ourselves been over his path, we could sympathize with the gaps in the narrative and the occasional confusion of place names and town positions. The mistake is excusable for many of the smaller settlements not only have names which sound alike, but their streets looked alike, felt alike and smelt alike. Luckily whenever the flow of Marco's tale dwindles into a vague trickle, the disciple is suddenly heartened by the intriguing mention of the Apples of Paradise or bitter bread; a puzzle becomes a challenge and the hunt is on for experiences which for any traveller past or present are liable to be etched deep into the memory.

Much more still remains to be studied about Marco Polo. The main substance of his work concerns Cathay itself and in order to do justice to Marco this part of his Journal needs careful comparative research. At least as a result of our journey it is possible to state that a close study of his descriptions of medieval Asia is worthwhile. The Marco Polo Route Project proved beyond all doubt that the fantastic tale of the *Description of the World* is no fanciful myth. It is a factual account whose detailed accuracy, even when viewed from a distance of six centuries, is remarkable. This increased confidence in the truth of Polo's writings can only be of great value. It provides a source of reliable data, a firm cross-reference for other accounts of thirteenth century Asia. Though Marco's description of his actual journey has never achieved the same recognition as his account of China, the story of his trail eastward along the caravan roads must therefore also take its place as an important document of travel.

Too often the famous Venetian's name has been no more than a vehicle for casual reference on generalities, inferring that his Journal is highly suspect. Now, it is apparent that the details within his narrative deserve closer attention. The hot baths he spoke of near Erzincan in Turkey and the silk at Yezd in Persia lead to further cross-checks with the works of other medieval travellers, for example the renowned Arab travellers. Most of all, the facts which Marco Polo provides of thirteenth century Turkey, Persia and Afghanistan are worthy of belief in their own right. In some strange way the medieval incredulity of Europe concerning the prodigies of the East has its legacy in the popular present-day misconception of Marco Polo. This scepticism has long outlasted the original doubt over particular statements in the Journal which modern scholarship has proved to be accurate in every way.

If, as the result of the Marco Polo Route Project, any last vestige of this popular misconception has been dispelled, then the Project in our eyes could be counted as a worthwhile effort. In launching and executing the venture, the expedition brought sacrifice as well as reward. For all three of us the preparation for the trip, however scanty, meant hard work which took precedence over our academic studies. This time and trouble would have been a criminal waste if our trip had failed miserably. At the outset we took a calculated risk in this, and once we had started we had no thought of turning back.

There could have been many reasons for failure: our poor mechanical skill, lack of motorcycling experience, over-hasty preparations, the absence of medical precautions and so forth. In the end, looking back on the entire journey, we were most extraordinarily lucky. Even the injury to my foot in the long run turned out to be a stroke of good fortune for it enabled us to double the amount of Polian research. All along, our heedless trust in our own good fortune, whatever the obstacles, was a mark of our self-confidence in a time when parents, sponsors and detractors all worried about our foolhardiness. In due course we surfaced safely because never were we concerned with the future.

From the very beginning the motorcycle experts had breathed fire and brimstone at our total ignorance of either riding or repairing the machines. As it turned out, the experience wrung from coaxing aged Austin Sevens into life with poultices of bent wire and insulating tape was far, far more applicable in the field than theoretical mechanics learnt at the laboratory desk, where nylon stockings are not generally suggested as air filters. To safeguard our health, kind experts drew up diet sheets and imposed strict disciplines with regard to clean food, regular medicines, and above all purified drinking water. At the end of the trip, all three of us had been forced to jettison such schemes. We drank direct from scum-covered ditches and gladly accepted whatever food was available in the meanest surroundings. Despite this, apart from the inevitable stomach disorders, we were hard, lean and fit at the end of our trip. Gradually we became acclimatized to the humblest conditions and then thrived contentedly. More abstemious European parties took immense precautions with their diet and health, until a chance error exposed a gap in their defences and the unfortunate victim was sent prostrate.

Manhandling a motorcycle across the broken terrain proved to be a far surer way of keeping fit than coddling oneself behind mosquito nets. In turn this fitness led to an even greater understanding of the people and places we visited. Across all Asia the European Embassies in the far-flung capitals dread the arrival of the scrounging globe-trotters who descend like locusts expecting to be gorged at someone else's expense because they have driven across a foreign country. For us, it was a source of pride that we would seek such help only when absolutely necessary. As a result we were much more inclined to cut ourselves away from the ties with our own European way of life. When a town was reached, we preferred to seek out a small local resthouse and stay there in the manner of the usual traders and travellers.

Besides its healthiness, motorcycle travel in these parts of the world produces a peculiar brand of self-sufficient pride which extended into our everyday lives. On a motorcycle one is involved much more intimately with the physical challenges of crossing the countryside. This feeling of self-help tinges one's human associations. For example, if we were pushed around in some village by the local bully as sometimes happened, we were quite liable to push back, to the evident surprise of our tormentor. For the same reason we did not feel quite so alien to the local population as might be expected. If one has laboriously bumped along a dusty sidetrack past the peasants tending their flocks and fields, the local village becomes a natural and expected goal. One climbs off the motorcycle in the central square as if it were the most normal thing in the world. The teahouse, police station or bakery are as familiar as if one lived in the village. For this reason we never felt that we had descended from another planet, and could approach every situation with assurance. By the end of our trip, this relaxed approach had become so ingrained that it was embarrassingly difficult to break. On one memorable occasion at our first dinner aboard the ship out of Bombay, all three of us so far forgot ourselves as to pick up our plates and sniff the food suspiciously!

In reviewing the course of the trip, one error stands out clearly in what we did. There is no doubt that in the beginning we took with us far too much equipment which subsequently proved unnecessary. This may be surprising in view of the fact that our carrying capacity was limited to only two sidecars and motorcycles. Nevertheless our trail to the Eastern border of Turkey was littered with jetsam. It must be said that these discarded items, like sunglasses and cutlery, had served their purpose in letting us down gently to a more rugged, simple life. Our initiation came about by easy stages as the gradual disintegration of our transport taught us to do without such semi-luxuries. The real waste was the precious time which we spent in the first place, collecting these inessentials. The key to the problem must surely be to draw up a short list of real essentials (and it is surprising how few things are really needed) and then decide whether finances allow for secondary requirements like sleeping bags and handkerchiefs.

There was one thing however which all three of us missed sorely and about which we could have made no provision; the lack of books. It was if our minds had developed a muscle for reading and if we had no books the muscle got cramp. We certainly did not need books as a form of escape from our environment, which was sometimes harshly unpleasant. Rather, we felt as if our store of intellectual food had been depleted and needed replenishing like a camel's hump. To this end it was debatable whether after an arduous month on the trip we looked forward more to a bath and clean sheets or to the wallowing luxury of a good book. Certainly, during the journey itself a battered novel kindly donated by a chance-met expatriate was a prized possession.

One of the most frequent questions which we were asked about the Marco Polo Route Project was the cost of mounting such an expedition. This is a very difficult question to answer precisely. In the first place it would be fatal to organize such a trip with constant reference to the amount of money it will cost. There is no possible way of budgeting for the unexpected eventualities that may occur amid the peaks of the Hindu Kush. Also there is no possible way of knowing how cheaply one can survive until poverty forces one into the lowest scale of native life. Broadly speaking, the method that the Route Project employed was that two of us had £100 to spare and we put this money in a communal fund. Everything else would have to be met either through the generosity of various sponsors or through our own efforts at writing for newspapers and magazines. In the end the total theoretical expenditure of the journey including the fare back to England amounted to almost £2000. Beyond our original £200 we had nothing; it was the overwhelming generosity of our sponsors who saw us through to the end.

Reflections

In a sense the Marco Polo Route Project is a venture and an idea that is not yet finished. Before us still lies the Forbidden Corridor of the Wakhan and on the other side of the High Pamir waits the awesome magic of China. But at least we had originally set out to follow in the footsteps of Marco Polo Il Milione, using his Journal as our Guide. This we had done to the best of our ability, thereby vindicating the Epilogue of the *Description of the World,* where it is written :—

There was never any man yet, whether Christian or Saracen, Tartar or Pagan, who explored so much of the world as Messer Marco, son of Messer Nicolo Polo, Great and Noble Citizen of the City of Venice.

THANKS BE TO GOD
AMEN